THE VIDEO GAME PRODUCER
BY CASEY JAMES DAY

The Video Game Producer

By Casey James Day

© 2025 Bird Fight Press

Disclaimer

This book is a work of nonfiction, but some names, dates, stories, organizations, and identifying details have been changed to protect the privacy of individuals and/or companies. The views, reflections, and interpretations expressed are those of the author alone and do not represent the views of any company or organization. Quotations and references to other works are used for commentary, analysis, and educational purposes. Every effort has been made to properly credit sources, and any errors or omissions are unintentional. This publication is intended for informational purposes only and does not constitute professional advice. Readers should exercise their own judgment when applying concepts to real-world situations.

Published by:
Bird Fight Press
San Diego, 91977 CA, USA

Cover Design: Michael Montemarano

A CIP record for this book is available from the Library of Congress Cataloging-in-Publication Data

ISBN: 979-8-9943776-1-1 Ebook
ISBN: 979-8-9943776-0-4 Hardcover
ISBN: 979-8-9943776-2-8 Paperback

Printed in USA

CHAPTERS

Dedicated to

My Bash Bro,

Evan Perez

And

My Best Friend,

Jason Nicols

FOREWORD

By Josh Watson

When I began working in games, I was... *skeptical* about production.

To me, the "real work," the creative work, happened in design docs, concept art, prototypes, and playtests. As a designer, my world was iteration, experimentation, the push and pull that came with creating something from nothing. Production always felt like the opposite of that. Where creators chased possibility, I thought producers sought control.

I had convinced myself that creativity and structure lived on opposite ends of a spectrum, and that the more of one you had, the less of the other you got.

It is a familiar stance, especially for those new to the industry. You come in wanting to build, to make, to shape worlds out of ideas. The last thing you want is someone telling you what cannot be done. To a young developer, a producer can seem like the wall between vision and reality, the person who keeps you tethered to deadlines when your head is still in the clouds.

That is where I was when I met Casey Day. We met while working on *Rocket League*, a game that had exploded far beyond anyone's expectations. At a studio where any creative idea was possible, and we were encouraged to think wildly to push the boundaries around what the game *could* be. It was also one of those rare projects that shifts overnight from a small team's passion to a live service behemoth with tens of millions of players and infinite moving parts. The kind of environment where production either holds everything together or completely collapses under its own weight.

At the time, I was a fresh-faced game designer and did not think I needed a producer. What I needed, apparently, was perspective.

Casey wasn't like the producers I had worked with before. He led with a flexibility rooted in his own curiosity. He didn't just ask for tasks and estimations; he would inquire about why we were making it in the first place. He wanted to understand how things affected the game and our players, not just how they were tracked. There was a patience and appreciation for the craft that made you want to meet him halfway.

As you grow and spend enough time in development, you start to realize that good production is the gravitational force that holds everything together. When it is off, even slightly, the orbit of the entire project shifts. Many producers try to artificially create that gravity with an abundance of process. Casey did it with alignment. He had a quiet ability to reframe problems so that people could see them the same way.

His impact was subtle at first, like the way he would lighten the tone of a meeting or use his curiosity to drive two teams that had been talking past each other for weeks toward a clear plan. But over time, I started to see it everywhere.

That was when I began to understand the difference between task management and leadership.

Casey uses this phrase throughout the book that boils down to: "A good producer is a force multiplier." At first, it sounds like one of those buzz phrases you hear in corporate environments. But when you watch him work, man... it fits. He didn't make things happen by pushing the team harder. He built systems that allowed other people to move faster. He created efficiency rooted in empathy to positively impact the product and our team.

That was the shift for me.

Until then, I thought production was about process. Casey showed me it is about people. It is about creating an environment where good ideas don't die from friction. Where artists, engineers, and designers aren't fighting each other's constraints but feeding each other's momentum. And at its core, production is not about managing creativity, it enables it.

That philosophy changed the way I lead teams as a Game Director. I let go of that naive view that saw structure as the enemy of imagination and started seeing it as its foundation. The right systems give the most ambitious ideas the opportunity to exist.

Casey builds those systems instinctively. He knows when to introduce just enough structure to bring clarity without slowing progress, and he understands that leadership isn't about authority. It's about alignment.

His unique mindset is captured within this book.

The Video Game Producer isn't a manual or a checklist to be mindlessly ticked. It's a reflection of the way Casey thinks and the way he turns our experiences into frameworks anyone can use. In the same way that Casey changed my perspective of the producer, this book reframes how we talk about production; not as a discipline that manages games, but as one that nurtures them.

Every chapter in this book comes from a place of lived

experience, and each story connects the lessons so many of us learn as gamers to the lessons we need as developers. It connects the same skills that make someone a good player — awareness, adaptability, communication — to the foundations of becoming a good producer. Casey's gift is showing how those skills intersect.

This book isn't just for producers. It's for anyone who wants to understand how teams actually work. It's for designers who want to communicate better, for engineers who want to see the bigger picture, and for leaders who want to build environments that last. It's for anyone who's ever felt the pull between creativity and control and wondered if the two can coexist.

If you come into this book... *skeptical*, I understand. I started there too. But keep reading. Let Casey's perspective challenge yours. Because if you give it a chance, you will see what I did.

FORGED THROUGH GAMES

I consider myself lucky to have grown up in the golden era of 90s gaming. Sure, the generations before me had their own defining moments: arcade halls in the 70s, and the rise of home consoles in the 80s. But, 90s kids got to experience something entirely new. We got the internet.

We were given front-row seats to witness several layers of gaming culture evolve before our eyes. As a kid, I was shouting at a split-screen TV with my friends on the living room couch, passing around a shared controller. Then, dial-up internet via AOL "Free Trial Disks" opened up a gateway into a whole new world. I was able to connect with thousands of other gamers all online at the same time. I will never forget the screeching sounds of the modem trying to connect to the internet and anxiously waiting for the satisfying alert, "You've Got Mail!"

I was one of those kids who fell in love with online gaming. I would fall asleep every night thinking about the games I had played, strategizing creative new ways to beat them, and looking forward to the new players I might come across. Every match I played honed my ability to work with others. Every challenge forced me to think critically and solve problems under pressure so that I could win. It was something I felt I was good at, but I never met a parent or another adult who thought the same way.

Despite all the strategy and teamwork involved, most people from previous generations still do not see the connection between gaming and the application of those skills outside of gaming. They treat games as entertainment, and not as a training ground on which you can develop or practice skills. Moreover, some players feel like they have confidence and leadership when they are playing games, but feel that the real world is completely alien to them.

I see it as a two-for-one deal. Video games do more than entertain because they build real skills that can shape careers. Project management and leadership are two great examples of these skills, but gaming fosters many more abilities that can fit into any industry or company. I might be biased, as I am now a Video Game Producer, but it makes sense to me to use lessons from video gaming to help foster these skills and their transition to the real world.

While I never stopped gaming, I eventually grew up and took my gaming skills into the workforce. I spent a few years in the Marine Corps as an aviation electrician, where I saw leadership in action first-hand. But I see the same amount of value, or even more, from experiencing digital strategy and leadership in games. After the military, when I transitioned to the games industry, I thought there could be better ways to show other gamers that real-world leadership and digital leadership are extremely similar and have an incredible crossover value. I've since worked across the industry, from AAA studios to indie start-ups, and I've worked on many different genres of games. I've been on teams that have developed for mobile, PlayStation, Xbox, Nintendo, and PC platforms. These skills I've developed throughout my career are universal.

The best parts of this journey are having a satisfying, fulfilling career in which to continue honing those early skills I learned from games, find ways to apply them to my teams, and teach the younger generations entering the workforce. My goal as a video game producer has been to break previous generational biases and embrace video games as a tool for learning. And I'm willing to bet, if you've got this book in your hand, you've been developing similar skills throughout your years of gaming that are just waiting to be applied to your daily lives and careers.

If you are still with me, let's take a look at two types of critical skills gamers have nowadays, called technical and strategic abilities. Some gamers can move their mouse or controller at lightning speeds to aim with pinpoint accuracy. They can quickly execute different button combinations to pull off cool moves in-game. Those could be classified as technical gaming skills. Then there are the strategic players who are helping with communication and teamwork, trying to lead and give their teammates a better chance at success. This kind of planning and managing could be considered strategic skills. In professional industries, and especially as a video game producer in the games industry, those technical and strategic abilities are called soft and hard skills.

Hard skills *are the technical aspects of a job, the actual process or work being performed.*

Soft skills *involve communication, teamwork, and how we interact with others.*

Both skill sets are important, yet many people evaluate success in the workplace by first measuring hard skills. Just like in video games, people measure success by the highest scores or the fastest times. In reality, soft skills like communication and relationships with your team have the biggest impact.

This discrepancy in value can also be seen in how we label these skills. Calling something a soft skill makes it seem optional when it's often the glue holding a team together. A video game producer can't rely on technical knowledge alone. The soft skills of leading a team, making decisions, and keeping a project on course are just as, and often more, critical. I want to reframe these ideas to show what really drives success.

One of the biggest shifts I want to encourage with this book is to change how my industry values certain skills. Hard skills, such as programming or character design, often get all the attention because they are easier to see, but soft skills are far more vital to the success of a project and a company. It's time to move past outdated ideas and recognize what truly drives success.

As video game producers, our work is rooted in project management, but the leadership trait is required. Throughout this book, we will explore project management concepts from a gamer's perspective and encourage the shifts in perception that can make us effective producers. Let's start by replacing the idea of soft skills with the concept of Leadership. And the concept of Managing will replace the idea of hard skills. Hold your horses if you think you understand the terms Leadership and Management, because I have a specific take on what I mean by them, which I will discuss in the upcoming sections. These shifts in perception are at the core of what I believe it means to be a Video Game Producer.

Every section of this book begins with a video game story, experience, or design concept, which leads into key principles that make the lessons clear and practical for gamers. Everyone should be able to relate to some of these games or the types of genres they fall under. We start with leadership, formerly called soft skills, and why it's critical to understand before you can jump into the hard skills. Once those lessons and video game comparisons lay the groundwork for your understanding of leadership, then we try to apply it while managing the work.

The goal is to give you a clear understanding of what a video game producer does and how you can use your gaming experience to develop the skills needed for the role. Even if you don't want to be a video game producer, these skills are universal for anyone who just wants to lead and be efficient in any team environment. By the end, you will have a practical way to apply what you have learned, and will see how the games you play have already been training you this entire time. Enjoy!

PART ONE - THE FIRST STEP

In the early 2000s, *Counter-Strike* was more than just a game; it was the opportunity to make a name for yourself. This became a world of possibilities for a 13-year-old kid like me. My brothers and I, along with our closest friends, were regulars at our local cybercafe in Southern California, where the hum of PCs and the glow of CRT monitors created an atmosphere that felt alive. At the time, the top two games were *Diablo 2* and *Counter-Strike*. We spent countless hours there playing both of those games. The best part was that we got to experience it all together in person at the cybercafe.

Somehow, we had a natural talent for shooting games, so our game of choice was *Counter-Strike*. Our favorite thing to do was to challenge people locally at the LAN center because one undeniable truth was starting to emerge. We always won. No matter which team we were faced with, our raw talent put us ahead of everyone in town.

One day, my friend suggested we join a digital league to compete in *Counter-Strike*, which shows how big our egos had become. The **Cyber Athletic League (CAL)** launched in early 2001 with a single *Counter-Strike* division and 3,000 members. It quickly became a cornerstone of the rising online esports scene. By the time we discovered it, CAL had grown into a powerhouse, boasting around 300,000 registered members across the world.

Competing in the league and performing well was an opportunity for sponsorships and fame. CAL was creating some of the first professional video game tournaments, where millions of dollars in prizes were at stake. As kids, we got to see those early players pave the way to being able to make a living from gaming. With stars in our eyes, we quickly jumped onto our computer to sign up and register our first team. As we filled out the digital application and entered our information, a simple step turned into our first major challenge.

We had to decide who would take on the role of leader.

Instinctively, we handed the title to Brad, our most skilled player. The best players are always the ones who lead the team. Who hasn't seen an American football movie where the high school quarterback is the best on the team and the natural leader?

We soon learned a harsh truth. Somehow, raw video game shooting talent didn't equate to effective leadership.

In CAL, the leader's responsibilities extended far beyond who could fire at an opponent's head the fastest; they also included administrative duties. When the league matched you with an opposing team for the week, the leader had to communicate directly with that team to coordinate the match schedule. The leader was also responsible for submitting the results and scores after the game so CAL operations could update the ranks as quickly as possible. There was no automation to handle any of this stuff for us at the time.

Brad was an exceptional player and friend, but he wasn't interested in planning or admin work. His casual responses of "This is lame," or "I do not care what other people think," quickly became a barrier to our participation in the league.

His reluctance to compromise hit its final wall when scheduling our first match. Brad proposed a single date that worked for him, but refused to budge when the opposing team couldn't accommodate it. This stalemate threatened to cost us the match, as we risked forfeiting it due to our inability to just find a compromise.

Within just a week of forming our *Counter-Strike* team, the cracks were already starting to form. Brad's inbox was inundated with emails from other teams requesting match schedules for the upcoming weeks, and his frustration was growing exponentially.

The stars in our eyes were starting to fade as our ambitious dream began to unravel. "I don't know if I can keep this up," Brad admitted, throwing his hands up in frustration.

For me, the idea of being a leader wasn't that hard to grasp. Years of playing team sports like football and soccer had shown me the importance of organization and coordination. Looking back, I realized that, in those leagues, it had been the adults who handled the heavy lifting. Parents ran the leagues, organized practices, and ensured we had the equipment we needed to train each day.

Our situation was completely different now.

CAL was a self-organizing league. For the first time, no coach or parent was stepping in to handle the logistics for us. If we wanted to make this work, it was entirely on us to figure it out.

Brad wanted to step down, but without someone in the leader role, our team wouldn't last. I wasn't the team's best shooter, and I didn't have the most outgoing personality. In fact, at that age, I was shy and reserved. But I was determined to compete, and that motivated me to push past my own fears. So, despite the doubts swirling in my head, I volunteered. "I'll do it," I said. "I just want to compete."

That decision to step up marked the beginning of my intense crash course in leadership.

I quickly learned, as Brad had already discovered, that scheduling a match wasn't as simple as just picking a time. It required negotiation and constant communication with both my friends and the opposing squads. If one of my friends couldn't make a proposed time, I had to go back to the other team and renegotiate. It became a balancing act of everyone's personal commitments.

Managing a team wasn't just about setting match schedules. It was also about maintaining team morale and navigating the expectations of friends who now had a new label: "Teammate."

Since I knew when the matches would be scheduled, I was also in the best position to plan the team's practices. We agreed to practice at least once or twice a week before a match. I was soon juggling the availability of four friends, each with their own commitments, ranging from family obligations to "girlfriend nights." Despite our hectic schedules, I made sure we stuck to our practice schedule, competed in official matches, and remained friends.

Taking on the role of *Counter-Strike* team leader for my friends was one of the defining moments of my youth. It taught me that leadership comes in many forms, but is less about authority and more about serving others. It is less about the title of "Leader" and more about lifting others so that everyone gets to play.

What started as just a game became a lifelong lesson in teamwork and growth. Those experiences stayed with me, shaping how I navigate challenges both in and out of the industry.

This was my first step toward becoming a video game producer.

THE PRODUCER

What is a producer? This profession shares similarities and differences with the titles of project manager, program manager, and even film producer. In another context, I would gladly go into deeper detail about those roles, but for this book, we are going to focus on what we call the Video Game Producer.

In the game industry, producers don't contribute to a game by doing any of the work that you can see, hear, touch, or smell in the game itself. They don't write code that makes your character jump in the air. They don't make cool 3D art or models with stunning visual effects. They aren't making any designs of your favorite levels. So, what do they do?

Simply, they work with teams or individuals to find ways to make them work better. If we want official definitions, I've been heavily inspired by Ben Carcich, a podcast host and video game producer himself. He has a great take on the topic, and I have adjusted it to help fit this book and blend with my own interpretations of being a producer.

> A **Video Game Producer** *is a leadership role focused on managing sections of, or the entirety of, the game development process, to ensure the team's goals (shared vision) are reached. They act as a force multiplier to teams and individuals by creating systems that beneficially support and remove disruptions.*[1]

I know that sounds fancy, but it's less complicated than it looks. We will break this definition into each of its parts and analyze them within the context of a producer's job, but let's clarify some definitions right off the bat. When we say "a leadership role focused on managing," we need to distinguish the differences between leading and managing.

- **Leading** *emphasizes goal setting and creating culture by driving change.* It involves guiding the team through setting a cultural example of fostering collaboration and motivating individuals to contribute their best work toward the goals.

- **Managing** *focuses on creating consistent systems and modeling desired behaviors of game production.* As architects of those systems, they ensure that the process is sustainable, and they become a force multiplier of the efforts of the team.

To be an effective producer, you must do both. Leadership without management makes you a spectator in the stadium, rooting for your team. Management without leadership reduces

---

1   This quote is my own, but it was heavily inspired by the work of Ben Carcich. See: Carcich, B. (Host). (n.d.). *Building Better Games* Podcast. Retrieved January 30, 2025.

you to a simple task coordinator.

To be a video game producer, leadership is mandatory. Embrace it.

It's also critical to note that leading does not imply authoritarian power. Instead, it's about the actions themselves, how you treat others, and how working toward shared goals sets the behavioral standards for the team to follow. After all, you can't lead without followers.

Managing is often misunderstood as managing people, or being a literal "Manager." Oxford Dictionary defines it as *"having executive or supervisory control or authority."*[2] I intentionally avoid that language in my definitions because it emphasizes a negative, outdated aspect of being a producer. So, let's break this explanation down further to really define the details of these definitions.

For starters, what does it look like to emphasize goal setting?

Goals can be any type of objective you want to set for yourself or the team. In video game terms, the goal can be as broad as completing a game with 100% achievements or getting to a high rank in online play. For the producer, depending on the team, it could be as simple as getting a new level out to the players or as complex as launching an entirely new game.

This is where *creating a culture by driving change* comes into play with *goal setting*. As we set these goals, we create the culture that we think works best for us and our teams. For example, do we want our teams to have cultures that represent serious or casual work styles?

Both options are acceptable and can be fun to work in, but they

---

2   *Oxford English Dictionary Online*, s.v. "managing," retrieved January 30, 2025.

each have trade-offs.

A serious team might push for quick deadlines to get things done faster. They expect long work hours and have a singular focus on getting the job done. It's like a top-tier esports squad grinding away for a championship title. This approach could lead to burnout and additional stress if not managed well, but when done successfully, it can provide a powerful sense of momentum and lead to some very satisfying achievements.

On the other hand, a team with a casual culture might prioritize a healthier work-life balance. The focus is on social interaction and waiting to find the fun rather than just hitting deadlines. It's more like a community-driven MMO guild where enjoyment and consistency matter more than performance and results. As an industry, games are a business, and if you miss deadlines, there could be financial repercussions.

The producer plays a key role in shaping these cultures while keeping the goals in mind. Sometimes they don't set goals. Sometimes they don't set the rules. But they do enforce and reinforce the team's established direction.

Let's move on to the other parts of our definition of what a producer does. Producers become the architects of the *systems* for their teams and understand how to be a *force multiplier* for them.

Force multipliers and systems might sound complex, but think back to the earlier story about scheduling games for *Counter-Strike*. When a leader can accommodate everyone's commitments so that each individual doesn't have to personally worry about it, they are curating a simple yet powerful system. Video game producers create these kinds of solutions on a professional scale alongside their game development teams.

If you reflect on your previous gaming experiences, there are probably systems you've already built yourself. Think about games like *Minecraft* or Survival RPGs that use chests to organize loot and supplies. Once players acquire multiple chests, they run into the problem of, "Which chest was that in again?"

If there is no organization, it's hard to remember where you put your items. So, as players, we instinctively create processes, like building signs, to label chests for plants, mining resources, food, and so on. This is system-building. It's what producers do, only at a larger scale and in a game studio setting.

In game production, the term "system" is interchangeable with process. Producers are the owners of their team's **systems**, *that is, a set of principles or procedures according to which something is done; an organized framework or method.*[3]

As a video game producer, I use systems to schedule meetings, determine how often the team should meet, and define what should be discussed. I determine how work is tracked and organized, like the way those chests are labeled.

One of my first tasks as a producer was to organize and sort through new bugs the QA team had found. This was no small feat, as a QA team can encounter hundreds to thousands of bugs that come in many different shapes and sizes. There are different levels of priority and severity that need to be considered. Game-breaking bugs need to be a higher priority than slight map

---

3   *Oxford English Dictionary Online*, s.v. "system," retrieved January 30, 2025.

issues. I used a system of labels to organize these bugs, which created organized boxes that the dev team could pull from when they needed to work on one. A successful producer is one who can create consistent systems that the team wants to work in, because it makes the team more efficient.

If a system is consistently reliable, then you can expect the same results reliably as well. Let's go back to that *Minecraft* example: if the first box on the left is always plants, the middle box is always mining resources, and the right box is always food, then we have a consistent and reliable system, as long as it doesn't change.

As a player, instead of asking, "Which box has what in it?" You know for certain what each box is, at least by its category. And, you've saved yourself all the time it takes by not checking the wrong box.

Now, you can get what you need and go back to playing the game for fun.

However, it's important to note that when you create systems, there is a possibility that they will fail and cause the opposite effect, which would be a disruption. We aim for *systems that beneficially support and remove disruptions.*

Removing disruptions, especially time-wasting ones, is crucial because a producer's job is to facilitate productivity rather than hinder it. For instance, if you create a system with many different types of chests that require the player to run back and forth, and it is hard to remember where each item goes, that would be a disruption, not an optimization.

If this is all done correctly, let's say we have just the right number of boxes to store all the loot, and everything is located in the most convenient spot for anyone to reach. Everyone is putting items where they belong in the correct boxes. No one is complaining about their time being wasted while managing their inventory. And, at the end of the day, everyone is having more fun than before. Those are examples of preventing disruptions and being a force multiplier within your systems.

These two concepts are at the heart of what it means to be an effective producer: a video game producer exercises leadership through goal-setting and culture change, and manages as a force multiplier through system building. When you get a job in the games industry and apply these two concepts together, you will be considered highly valuable for any team you join.

A producer's first task might be organizing the work for the team you are assigned to. Production Coordinators and Associate Producers (known as APs) are entry-level roles in game production, and they are usually brought in for these types of task organization. This was my first role, as I mentioned in the story above, where I had to sort, organize, and label QA bugs to put them in the correct boxes. Other producers might be sorting, organizing, and labeling upcoming work, and instead of putting them in boxes, they are assigning them directly to their teams.

As a producer gains more experience, they can be promoted and take on more responsibilities, which in turn allows them to create more complex systems that impact more team members and the other producers they work with. As you grow to work on bigger systems across teams, you start to coordinate with other producers. This creates a vital intersection of workflows that requires you to understand your fellow producers, their focus, systems, and who they are leading.

Most departments are set up hierarchically, with teams reporting to managers and so on, until you reach the leadership at the top. It doesn't matter if it's the Art, Engineering, Audio, or Design department; the production hierarchy is usually the same. The coordinators, APs, and producers might support individual teams within the art department, such as the Concept Team, Animation Team, or 3D Modeling Team. Then, Sr. Producers might manage the entire Art Department, including each individual team with its own assigned producers.

As you move up through departments, the entire game management might be run by an Executive Producer or a Director of Production. When you get to the Director and Executive level, you also have more responsibility to create systems that are force multipliers for the other producers under you. These high-level roles have a massive influence and usually set the tactics and standards for all the other producers who work under them.

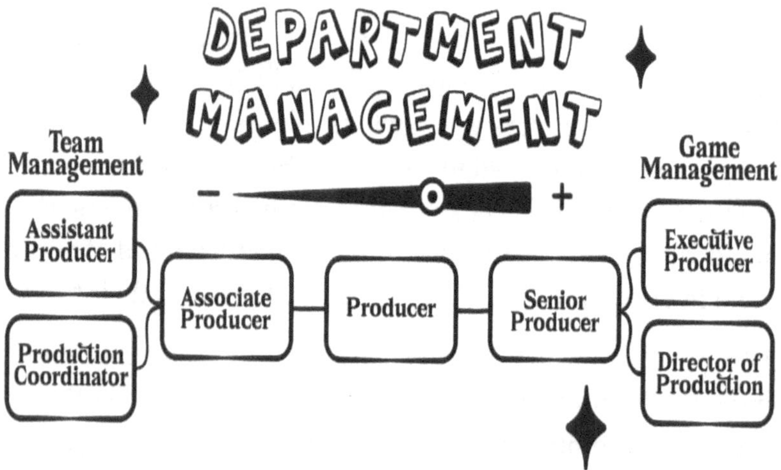

This hierarchy of producer roles is not absolute. It depends on the team's size and structure, and in the AAA games industry, this hierarchy continues to evolve. In the image below, you can see a clear breakdown of the different producer roles. The roles on the left have less management, and the roles to the right have more management and responsibility to consider.

Do not be misled by this straightforward chart, though, as there are always exceptions. Understanding that there is no one-size-fits-all approach to being a producer in the games industry is key. As a highly technical field, the video game industry is always changing, so it is important to stay up to date with its current needs and workflows.

I have seen the title of Producer grow from just "Producer" to things like "Engine Producer," "Platform Producer," and now "AI Producer." At one studio I worked at, every producer was just called "Producer," regardless of their role or what department they worked for. The studio leads thought that it wasn't important how senior or junior you were; a producer is just a producer. I have also seen video game studios where they don't hire producers at all, as the function of leading and managing was handled by their department leads instead. Neither approach is wrong. It is just a decision made by different studios.

The point is that the industry and teams are ever-evolving, and we, as producers, must evolve with it.

But it wasn't always that way.

ORIGINS

In the early 1980s, video game production was a simpler affair and took place on a much smaller scale. Teams were small, often consisting of only a few people, with individuals shouldering multiple responsibilities. In some cases, a single developer handled everything. Sid Meier is a legendary developer who started his career with just a single business partner who handled the sales. They created *Hellcat Ace* in 1982, which became their first big success. Later, they led the development of *Civilization*, *Pirates!*, and *Railroad Tycoon* with teams that were small in comparison to today's standards.

Following his success as a solo developer, Sid brought on specialized team members, including artists and audio composers. As their games grew more complex, he leveraged their skills to handle specific areas of game development, so he could spend more time focusing on the technology behind their games.

This was a smart decision, as growing expectations for video games across the industry required technological advances. For example, the leap from 8-bit to 16-bit graphics opened the door to richer visuals, complex game mechanics, and deeper story-driven narratives. These advances made larger teams and specialized roles necessary.

From the start, engineers managed increasingly sophisticated code constrained by extreme memory limitations. Today's games, such as Fortnite and *Grand Theft Auto V*, have file sizes exceeding 100 GB. For comparison, the early game *Super Mario Bros.* had a memory size of 40KB, a difference akin to squeezing an entire library into a single book.

During this earlier period, game production remained informal, often driven by the passion of a director or a team member eager to take charge rather than a defined production process.

In 1982, another developer, Trip Hawkins, founded *Electronic Arts* (EA). It was around this time that he introduced the "Producer" role to video game development. As its name suggests, he modeled this role on record producers in the music industry, even bringing in producers from *A&M Records* to train EA's first video game producers.

The rise of 3D gaming in the late 1990s marked a turning point in the game production pipeline. Titles like *Super Mario 64* and *Tomb Raider* demonstrated the possibilities of 3D graphics, but also highlighted the steep rise in development costs. Unlike 2D games, where a small team could handle most of the work, 3D production requires specialized roles with higher technical demands. Animating characters instantly became more complex, programming movement required advanced physics and collision systems, and modeling environments demanded more time and computing power. Each of these developments increased the team size, the budget, and the need for communication across departments.

It was during this time that video game producers began to establish themselves as indispensable figures, orchestrating the many moving parts of a game's development.

By the early 2000s, the gaming industry had entered its blockbuster era, which many would call the birth of the AAA game. Titles like *Halo: Combat Evolved*, *World of Warcraft*, and *Grand Theft Auto III* were massive undertakings, involving hundreds of developers. The budgets of these games rivaled those of Hollywood films, which made the risks of blockbuster games higher than ever.

As teams grew and development pipelines expanded, production practices had to evolve rapidly to sustain costs. Video game producers became the conductors of these efforts, ensuring teams could communicate and share updates quickly.

In many ways, game development drew inspiration from filmmaking. Both industries share a focus on storytelling through a visual medium and rely on producers to manage workflows across teams. Unlike films, however, games are interactive and require constant testing for feedback and iteration. Keeping up with modern standards demands new technology and tools for the teams. This challenge led producers to adopt hybrid approaches, combining proven methods from different industries to tackle the complexities of game development.

Now a decades-old industry, game development is a global effort. Studios build games across multiple locations, with different teams handling various parts of development. I worked on *Rocket League,* a popular car soccer game where we did exactly this. Our main studio in San Diego focused on core mechanics and vehicle design. An art team in Europe created 3D models for those vehicles, including wheels and paint decals. A QA team in South America tested those assets to make sure they worked properly and were free of major bugs. Keeping this kind of process organized requires strong coordination, and that is where producers step in.

AAA studios rely on producers to manage this global pipeline. Each team, whether in art, engineering, or QA, will have a producer responsible for keeping their team's work on track. Those producers align their teams' schedules with the larger roadmap. A senior or executive producer then gathers those schedules into a full project plan. This structure helps break up the work and keep the teams accountable for specific information and plans.

On a smaller scale, indie studios handle production with fewer people and resources, but still face the same challenges as larger teams and studios. They must manage schedules, track progress, and coordinate across disciplines, perhaps without dedicated producers for each team. Some of those teams have a single producer overseeing development, while others share production-related tasks among the other developers.

Indie teams stay efficient and use the same tools as AAA studios, but adapt them to fit their needs.

Jira, *Trello*, and *Confluence* are digital tools that help track tasks, while version control systems like *Git* keep code organized. Large production pipelines require too much overhead, so indie teams focus on flexibility. Lightweight task-tracking boards (i.e., Kanban boards) and quick check-ins replace complex workflows, keeping development moving without unnecessary bottlenecks.

AAA studios rely on structured hierarchies to manage large teams across different disciplines, while indie teams take a more hands-on approach. A producer in a smaller studio might handle production alongside marketing and business tasks. Developers often step into multiple responsibilities, balancing their work with the demands of keeping a project on track. Instead of rigid structures, indie teams rely on problem-solving and efficiency to push projects forward.

The journey of game production is one of continuous evolution, from lone developers in the 80s to global teams shaping modern masterpieces. It's a story shaped by creative ideas and the determination to create experiences that players will talk about. Video game producers are the guides on this journey, ensuring that every player's experience is as memorable as the dream that inspired it.

LEADERSHIP'S VISION

The air was thick with tension as bullets ripped through the treeline, leaving behind a spray of bullet tracers and devastation. My squad was pinned down near the eastern edge of our next capture point. "Hold your positions," our squad leader's voice came through the channel, steady and controlled. "Don't peek. We're outnumbered. I'm calling for artillery and resupply."

This game was intense. The enemy fire forced us to stay crouched behind cover without a second of reprieve. We were pinned down, unable to move. I saw teammates peek up and instantly get shot by enemy bullets, followed by the call for medics. Despite the hectic nature of other players begging for medics, our leader's composure was steady. "Squad, prepare for a push. We're not leaving until we get to this point. Medics, get our wounded up." His confidence cut through the panic and snapped us to attention.

Switching to the command channel, his voice carried the same calm authority. "Command, this is Squad 4. We're under heavy fire on the eastern side of Objective Charlie. Can we get artillery support on the south treeline, where it's currently marked on the map? We'll also need a supply run after this push for more respawns."

The commander on the battlefield acknowledged his request. Moments later, artillery rumbled off in the distance, followed by the unmistakable explosions of rounds hitting their marks.

With a hint of amusement, our squad leader reported back to us: "Artillery's up... Get ready to advance on my mark."

The squad leader continued coordinating with straightforward instructions, "Suppress the treeline! Use smoke grenades! Push hard, no hesitation." It was motivating to see all of us following the same orders and pushing together, almost like a real army. We followed his lead, pushing forward as the enemy was slowly overwhelmed and started to fall back.

When we secured the point, the squad chat erupted with cheers, but he quickly refocused us, "Great job, everyone. Build up fortifications. We need to hold this ground. We don't know when the resupply from command is coming."

It didn't matter, because a few moments later, after we had reached the strategic objective, we defeated our enemy opponents by total points. They didn't have enough resources to respawn their team, so we won the game.

After the match, still riding the high of victory, I sent the squad leader a quick message to compliment his leadership and ask how he had become so experienced in the game. His reply was polite and modest, but one detail stopped me in my tracks. He was only 15 years old and had just started playing a couple of months earlier.

The way he was talking in-game, with all that composure, tactical knowledge, and the ability to coordinate multiple teams, was remarkable for his age. It was hard to reconcile how impressive that was, coming from someone too young to legally drive a car.

Sometimes, people show that leadership is not tied to age and wisdom; it's a skill that can be practiced. The game's mechanics and communication systems gave our squad leader the opportunity to magnify his ability to guide and inspire his teammates. But how did this translate to effective leadership?

Squad, developed by Offworld Industries in 2020, is a military simulation (Mil-Sim genre) that demands teamwork. The game's communication system forces players to rely on it through a hierarchy, like a real military unit would. Each Squad Member talks to their Squad Leader. Then each Squad Leader talks with the single Game Commander. All these roles are actually played by individual players.

However, authority means nothing in the digital world, so how do regular players lead other gamers without the real-world titles? Just because a game forms a structure or hierarchy between the players, it rarely means the players will listen to each other. This isn't a job where you have a boss and there are real-world consequences if you don't listen to them. Video games are a form of entertainment, and you volunteer your time when you play.

So when it does work, what are these leaders doing and why are other players following them?

Effective leadership is the same whether it's in-game or in real life: *it involves setting clear goals and maintaining a focus on outcomes.*

Let's understand this through the video games you play before comparing it to the role of a video game producer. In games where they give you the opportunity to lead (this can even happen in single-player games), they usually also provide a clear goal.

The game's genre or category often makes this goal self-evident. For example, in games like *Squad*, your goal is probably to capture a point or eliminate all enemies on the modern battlefield. In an RPG, if you play as any form of hero, you are probably trying to save the kingdom or your home village.

While the game provides a clear goal, the best part of gaming is that the player gets to determine their own tactics in achieving that goal. If you didn't have that, a game wouldn't be a game; it would be considered work.

Basically, in gaming, we get help with the first part of leading because everyone is already aligned with the same goals. The second half of leading is the tricky part, *maintaining a focus on outcomes*. Without knowing it, our brains are constantly doing this and applying what is simply called a **strategy**, *which is a plan of action or policy designed to maintain focus in order to achieve major or overall goal.*

In-game leaders are just providing a strategy for people to follow so everyone can achieve their overall (usually predefined) goals in the game. The young leader from *Squad* knew that we all wanted the same objective, and he envisioned and enacted a strategy to get us there. To

Structure of leading in-game

better understand this element of strategy, let's break down what he did into two concepts: Objectives and Tactics.

- **Objectives** are t*he things you need to do in order to achieve the goal.*

- **Tactics** are t*he methods by which you achieve your goals and objectives.*

The goal of every player in *Squad* is to win by highest score. Since capturing areas on the map is key to victory, teams naturally focus on moving together to secure each point. So the squad leader had somewhat of an advantage from the start. Because everyone was aligned with those goals, he simply had to call out certain objectives to keep everyone working in the same area at once.

While this was a simple act of leadership, the squad leader communicated our objectives by suggesting tactics rather than dictating them. When he gave the instruction, "Hold your positions," he did not micromanage where each player should be. And when he said, "Squad, prepare for a push," he trusted us to do so as we saw fit. Myself and the rest of the team could instantly understand how these objectives aligned with our universal goals, and it united us in our efforts.

When the objective is clear, the key to success is to be reasonable and logical in the tactics we use to get there. This comes down to communication. Often, it is better to communicate any objective rather than none, because with a reasonable goal, the team can apply their own tactics. Without that, it could be a free-for-all.

It's pretty cool that modern video games use game mechanics to make this kind of communication easy. For example, many games contain the mechanic of a "ping". Since we don't have the option to point in a direction, games give us the ability to click at a distant location and share that point with other players in the game.

Sometimes, a reasonable objective is just an arrow pointing at a location you need to attack, and video game players get it.

When reasonable requests align with the overall goal, like winning the game, most people will listen and follow the proposed strategy. If our squad leader had told me to push the objective by myself, I would have considered that not reasonable. But when the leader instead said, "Let's push this objective together to overtake the enemy," we all responded because that sounded fair and was aligned with the team's goals of working and playing together.

With strong direction, every team member understands the objectives without needing constant verbal leadership. Ask any team member what they are working toward, and they should have a clear answer. When challenges arise, the team already knows how to navigate them because every action aligns with the objective.

Before we continue, we need to clarify two terms that we will use for the types of leaders that exist in gaming genres. I want to clarify the differences and show the similarities with video game producers:

- **Squad Leader** - Represents leadership in shooting games like *Battlefield, Call of Duty, ARMA, Valorant, Overwatch,* and *Counter-Strike.*

- **Raid Leader** - Represents leadership in managing large MMO groups in games like *World of Warcraft, Destiny 2, Final Fantasy XIV,* and *Eve Online.*

ROLE	GOAL	OBJECTIVE	TACTIC
Squad Leader	Win on a battlefield with small team coordination.	Lead your team to the capture point and make sure the enemy team cannot retake it afterward.	Visual markers or pings on the map to show people where to defend specific points.
Raid Leader	Defeat a boss in a raid dungeon with large team coordination.	Defeat the raid in under three hours.	A step-by-step list of what monsters to kill and what monsters to avoid to be efficient in time.
Video Game Producer	Make a Video Game with a game development team.	Create a plan for a brand-new vehicle for players to use.	Verbal and written communication with the requirements listed

See, leadership is pretty simple, right? If you're still with me, let's get into some of the more difficult aspects of providing direction and leading others. Every example before this involved video games that are fairly straightforward. However, not all games have such clear objectives that are easy to align with. In other cases, a valid goal might not even be fair when proposed, as it will impact some players more negatively. How do we get past this?

As video game producers, it's our job to solve this problem and serve as the Raid Leaders for our game development teams. I experienced this very early on in my career while working with technical teams. We had to make decisions based on subjective data, and we often had to do this under the pressure of a time constraint. Should we worry about player inventories or focus on launcher issues? Both were important and affected the user experience in different ways. But the workloads might be vastly different, and the teams affected might have limited bandwidth.

When things are unclear or tasks are unfair, it will be hard to get a team to rally behind you.

In more complex situations, we can still mimic the fundamentals of leading in games by trying to understand the goals, objectives, and tactics the project is trying to convey.

Let's convert the strategy pyramid from earlier to represent what is required in game development. Now we have: vision, pillars, and core values.

Structure of leading as a video game producer

- **Video Game Vision** is the high-level, holistic goal for what the game *is* and what *experience* it aims to deliver.

- **Game Design Pillars** are foundational design principles that support the game vision and lay the structure for the core features, mechanics, or themes the team will prioritize.

- **Core Values** are the collaboration principles and team behaviors that lay the foundation of how the pillars and vision get done.

When we look at these together, we can see that they form the overall strategy for the game development teams. The actual strategies can vary drastically depending on the vision, pillars, and values of the game teams. Let's dive into it.

The overall vision for the game shouldn't be complex; it should be easy to understand. That is our job to define and communicate, and I think this quote, "Leadership is the capacity to translate vision into reality,"[4] by Warren G. Bennis that reinforces this. When we look at the games we are trying to make, the vision statement should be able to describe them in a short, simple way that gives them a sense of reality.

For example:

Deliver a fast-paced, online-competitive shooter where players feel the intensity of battle through dynamic, destructible environments powered by cutting-edge physics.

Or:

Create an epic action-adventure where players explore a vast, open world, solve environmental puzzles, battle powerful foes, and uncover secrets through freeform discovery and experimentation.

With a high-level vision established, we set the initial north star for the project, and we can start working on the design pillars that will support the vision and break it out further. As mentioned above, the pillars of a game vision shouldn't involve every possible factor. It's easier and more effective to stay focused on a few things. Let's use the first vision statement as an example and break it down into three game design pillars.

1. **Fast-Paced, High-Mobility Combat**
   Emphasize speed, movement, and fluid gunplay to create intense, adrenaline-fueled firefights.

2. **Dynamic, Destructible Environments**
   Let players alter the battlefield in real time, creating strategic opportunities and unpredictable outcomes. Mandatory for all in-combat environment objects.

3. **Creative Team Play**
   Support diverse roles, tools, and tactics that reward

---

4   Bennis, Warren G. (2009.) On Becoming a Leader. Basic Books.

coordination and inventive approaches to objectives.

The vision defines where we're going. The pillars define guard rails and direct the focus to the kind of game we are building. Then, we can create the core values that define how we work together to get there. These are the tactical and cultural principles that shape our decisions, workflow, and creative process.

Example Core Values:

- **Clarity over control**
  Communicate intent clearly so teams can act independently and make aligned decisions.

- **Prototype first, polish later**
  Focus on validating the core fun before refining or scaling. Get hands-on quickly.

- **Fail fast, learn faster**
  Treat iteration as discovery. Test assumptions early and adapt quickly.

- **Player-first thinking**
  Every decision should trace back to player experience, not just features or technology.

With these defined, we can implement our game development strategy. If the problem of uncertainty or a lack of clarity arises, having these pillars and values defined is how you rally your team behind the strategy. When you give directions or try to lead the project, it will be easier because everyone is aligned with why they are doing it this way, just as our squad leader earlier led us toward the game's goals and objectives. It's simple and straightforward because they have broken it down as such.

Now, not all visions and pillars need to be that well-established at every level; you can manage with a high-level approach. At the individual department or team level, you can also create additional team visions or pillars to lead within that team. Yes, you can have visions at the game development level and visions at the team level as well.

When I was working on *Rocket League*, the overall vision for the game was defined as "a physics-driven, competitive sports game that doesn't take itself too seriously." *Rocket League* is an online soccer game with a twist: players drive rocket-powered cars instead of avatars and try to drive into the ball to score by knocking it into the opposing team's goal. The "don't take yourself too seriously" vision was applied in several beautiful ways, such as the art team making silly or ridiculous hats for players to unlock and use to dress up their cars.

My first assigned role on *Rocket League* was working with the publishing department. There was an individual team that I helped lead, which they called the Creative Services. That team handled all the key art and amazing screenshots of the game: the ones you see on blogs or websites showing off the latest updates to the game.

When I first joined them, I noticed they didn't have an individual vision or defined pillars to follow, so I helped create them, as the producer should if you haven't picked up on that already. This takes time, but it starts with conversations to find alignment within the team.

This is what the team's leadership agreed to:

- The vision of the Creative Services Team was to always highlight *Rocket League's* physics-driven and competitive gameplay, with a hint of silliness.

- We would communicate goals and outcomes when requesting content, but decided that the directions we gave to the artists and designers were to express their creative freedom in a way that supported the overall vision.

- We made sure our tactics weren't about micromanaging, but letting the team propose a concept they wanted. If that got approved, we wouldn't check back in to review until they were done.

You might have noticed something interesting here. These visions were about the team, not just the product or the game itself. These visions also applied to the internal game development team and to any other team that relied on creativity and content creation. Not all visions need to be just about progress; they can also be about the team's well-being.

So, with a strategy in place at the game or team level that has a vision, pillars, and core values written out, leadership is back to sounding easy. How do leaders still fail, then? The first complication to check for would be to see if the different teams have multiple visions. Are these visions aligned together and not competing against each other? If teams and companies can't align around a vision they all agree on, it will never become a shared vision. A **Shared Vision** *is a collective agreement and commitment from the entire team on what the vision should be.*

A vision is easy to agree on when it's one individual or a small group of individuals maintaining it, but to get the entire team bought on, it is mandatory to ensure the vision is a shared vision.

It does not matter whether you are working in a game studio, a corporate team, or a nonprofit organization. If people have a shared understanding of why they are working together, they have a shared vision. Decision-making becomes easier when the purpose is clear, and every action has meaning.

When a shared vision is missing or misaligned between the team, your job as a producer is to facilitate conversations and help the team find alignment. A lack of vision doesn't need to be a dead end. It is an opportunity to bring clarity where it is needed.

As a video game producer, you can schedule a meeting and talk about it. Address the elephant in the room. If you feel like there is no clear vision, say so. Have conversations to discuss this problem and see if others agree. A simple way to check alignment is to state what you believe the vision is. If others agree, then you are in sync.

If someone has a different vision, figure out why you are misaligned. Ask questions. Seek clarity. Talk it out. Start from the top down and ask the Executive Producers or Technical Directors on the team the following questions, or something similar:

> What is the most important thing we are trying to do with this game?
>
> Is it meant to be fun?
>
> Is it designed to make money?
>
> Is it supposed to make players cry?
>
> Is it meant to keep them consistently engaged, or is it for short sessions?

Start with the big picture and build from there. Creating and maintaining a shared vision is not without challenges. Differences in priorities or communication gaps can lead to misalignment. The challenge with a shared vision is that it must work for *everyone*. Teams are made up of people with different perspectives and experiences. The key is to avoid a weak vision. A weak vision does not align with anyone, no matter how many steps you follow to create it.

Now, this is where great leaders and bad leaders are made: if you are unable to facilitate and achieve alignment within the team, you will be stuck in the mud, going nowhere. That is why the next step in understanding leadership is about **Servant Leadership**. Servant leadership is the key to being an effective leader in any setting. Whether guiding a game development team, leading a squad on the battlefield, or organizing a raid group in an MMO, the same principle applies. Leadership is not about standing above others. It is about lifting them up. The best leaders serve their team's vision and do everything possible to help them succeed. In the next section, we will explore servant leadership in detail and see why it is the model that all leaders, whether in games or real life, should strive to follow.

SERVANT LEADERSHIP

Have you ever played a MOBA? Most people don't actually know what MOBA stands for. It's an acronym for **Multiplayer Online Battle Arena**. This genre is built around tactical, team-based gameplay, usually featuring between 6 and 12 players. The two biggest MOBAs in the world right now are *League of Legends* and *Dota 2*. While MOBA might be the coolest name for a genre, what makes this game type even more fascinating is its origin.

The first MOBA didn't start in a traditional game development studio with a game designer. It was born from the *Warcraft III* custom-games community. A modder, known as Eul, created a custom game called *Defense of the Ancients (DotA)*, modifying the existing Warcraft game to introduce a brand-new experience. *DotA* exploded in popularity to the point where people were buying *Warcraft III* just to play this custom game mode. It wasn't an official product; it was just something built by a dedicated fan.

Over time, other developers picked it up. Guinsoo, and later IceFrog, refined *DotA* into the version that laid the foundation for *Dota 2*. Meanwhile, *League of Legends* emerged as a spiritual successor, developed by *Riot Games* with its own spin on the formula.

For my brothers and friends, this quickly became another game to obsess over. For us, *League of Legends* had the perfect blend of teamwork, competition, and skill expression. It was a game with a simple premise, but it demanded team coordination.

League of Legends is played in two teams of five, each protecting their base while trying to destroy the enemy's. The game map is divided into three lanes that each lead to the opponent's base, and every player has a specific role that shapes how and where they play. Lastly, the player gets to choose their own champions with well over 100+ options to choose from with unique abilities, strengths, and weaknesses. The **meta**, *the normal or most current playing style*, in the game followed this structure, depending on what part of the map you played on:

- **Top Lane** was typically played by champions built for durability or sustained fights.

- **Middle Lane** was home to champions that would deal in magic damage.

- **Bottom Lane** was the only lane with two players who had different roles. One played the **ADC (Attack Damage Carry)** and focused on dealing damage over time. The other played **Support,** who ensured the ADC could farm safely and scale into the later stages of the game.

- **Jungle** was played by a champion who did not stay in a lane. Junglers looked for opportunities to help teammates by ambushing enemy players.

With five options to choose from, my group decided I would play Support in the bottom lane with my brother, who would be ADC (Attack Damage Carry).

This wasn't a suggestion. It was a decision made for me. Support was the beginner role, the one given to the person who

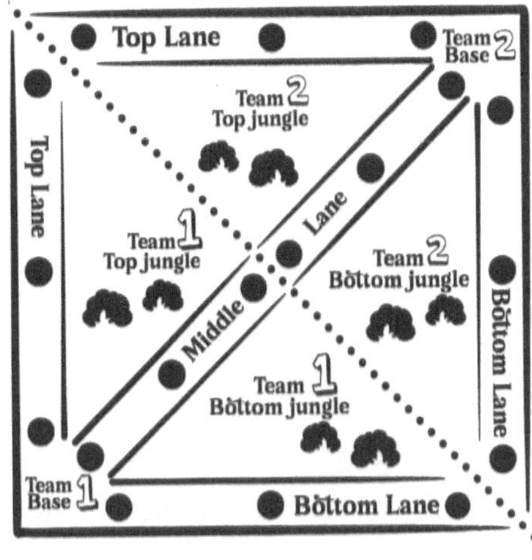

couldn't be trusted to handle a lane on their own. I was told to stay next to the ADC, heal them, and never leave their side. "Your job is to keep me alive. If I die, it's your fault." That was how my brother explained it to me.

At first, I accepted it. My job was simple. Heal when life is low. Shield to prevent oncoming damage. And make sure my ADC could farm without getting harassed. My go-to champion was Soraka, the easiest healer in the game. She had almost no damage, but she didn't need any. All I had to do was press a button to heal other champions and watch my teammates' health bars go back up. From my point of view, I wasn't making plays or deciding fights. I was the extra guy needed to fill a slot. What I didn't realize was that Support wasn't as simple as they made it sound. Every time we faced the opposing enemy ADC and their Support partners, I started noticing something.

Their Support wasn't always glued to their side, just healing.

Sometimes they would roam to other parts of the map, set up plays on the other lanes, or make sure the team had extra vision in the jungle area so they could see threats sooner. In each game, the enemy player in the Support role seemed to play differently, adjusting their tactics based on what their team needed. I realized that different Support champions could bring different advantages. Some could lock down enemies, holding them in place so our ADC could get a kill and earn more gold. Others roamed to different lanes, setting up fights before the enemy team even saw them coming. Some focused on disrupting the other team entirely, throwing them off balance at key moments.

It became clear that the Support role wasn't just about playing defensively anymore. It was about reading the game from all the lanes, knowing when to stay, when to move, and when to take control. The best Support players weren't just protecting one ADC. They were projecting and creating opportunities for the entire team to win together.

Once I understood that concept, my mindset about how I was supposed to play shifted immediately. I stopped picking champions based on who could just heal. Instead, I started choosing who would help us win.

If we needed a defensive wall type champion, I'd pick a tanky Support like Braum. He was a champion who could soak up damage and protect the team with a giant shield, and help with crowd control.

If our team lacked a way to start fights, I'd choose a champion like Thresh. He had a hook ability that could latch onto an enemy and pull them in closer, preventing them from escaping to set up an easy kill for the ADC.

What I came to realize was that teams that won in *League of Legends* weren't just the ones with the strongest players or the ones dealing the most damage. The teams that succeeded were the ones that synergized around the problem space, where every role complemented the others. A well-timed heal could save a fight before it even started. A stun at the right moment could secure a kill that changed the momentum of the game. Positioning and vision control made sure the team had an advantage and could take fights on their terms.

Unintentionally and without realizing it, we all started to play differently.

Once we understood that we wanted to help each other and find synergies that worked well together, the conversation shifted. Instead of asking, "How can I, as support, play and help?" We began discussing our strategy differently: "Who are the five champions that work best together?" Support roles are often the unsung heroes of video game leadership, secretly embodying a principle known as servant leadership.

This concept is widely recognized and applied in game development frameworks like the Scrum process, which we'll explore in later sections. It is also a term widely used in the corporate industry, which I personally believe is oxymoronic. The idea of using the word 'servant' is so demeaning, and it doesn't make it better by pairing it with 'leadership'.

However, to truly understand what it means to support a team and how to teach teams to support each other, you first need to understand the origins of servant leadership.

Robert K. Greenleaf, a pioneering thinker and corporate executive at AT&T, says it best: "The servant-leader is servant first... It begins with the natural feeling that one wants to serve, to serve first. Then conscious choice brings one to aspire to lead."[5]

---

5   Greenleaf, R. (n.d.). What is Servant Leadership. Greenleaf Center for Servant Leadership.

Best known for coining the term, Robert K. Greenleaf defined **Servant Leadership** *as a non-traditional leadership philosophy embedded in a set of behaviors and practices that place the primary emphasis on the well-being of those being served.*

Hermann Hesse's short story, *Journey to the East,* inspired Greenleaf's approach to leadership. In this symbolic tale, a group of travelers embarks on a spiritual journey supported by a humble servant named Leo. Leo performs small but essential tasks like cleaning, cooking, and tending to the animals, quietly guiding the group with his steady presence. Unfortunately, when Leo unexpectedly disappears, the group falls into disarray.

It is only later revealed that Leo was not merely a servant but the true leader of the secret organization that originally contracted the travelers, and it was his selfless service that held everything together.

This story deeply resonated with Greenleaf, sparking his belief that the best leaders lead by serving others. To him, leadership was not about wielding authority but about creating an environment in which individuals could grow and collaborate. Leaders, like Leo, become the unseen rope that ties teams together. They prioritize serving the team and looking out for their needs as they work toward a goal rather than controlling them and telling them what to do.

In the story, Leo noticed that the travelers on the trip were so tired, they weren't taking care of each other. He saw he could provide the most value and assistance through cooking and cleaning for them. Imagine how high morale can rise with clean clothes and a full belly. In their ignorance, they assumed he was lower-ranked than they were, as they associated his responsibilities with his level of respect. They never thanked or appreciated his help, and in the story he leaves them.

Greenleaf highlighted his philosophy of servant leadership in essays that explore the foundations of power and service. His research and visions inspired a set of actionable principles: the *10 Pillars of Servant Leadership.*

Let's add our own twist. Below, we explore the definitions of the original traits, but I have crafted them to apply to producers in game development and game leaders in competitive and cooperative gaming contexts as well.

10 Pillars of Servant Leadership for Producers & Game Leaders

Pillar	Description	Game Leaders	Producer
Listening	Actively seeks to understand team needs and concerns.	A Squad Leader listens to teammates' concerns about strategy and adjusts the plan.	A Producer prioritizes feedback from QA testers to identify and resolve key issues.
Empathy	Recognizes and addresses challenges faced by the team.	A Raid Leader notices a player struggling and pairs them with an experienced mentor.	Supports a designer struggling during a crunch by adjusting deadlines.
Healing	Helps team recover and improve after setbacks.	After a tough raid failure, the Raid Leader reframes it as a learning opportunity.	Leads a post-mortem after a failed milestone to strengthen future workflows.
Awareness	Maintains a holistic view of team dynamics and goals.	A Squad Leader senses low morale and boosts motivation with a team rally.	Recognizes a breakdown in communication between the art and engineering teams early.
Persuasion	Fosters alignment through dialogue, not authority.	Convinces a raid team to take on a tougher strategy that will yield better results.	Gains buy-in from stakeholders for a risky, but valuable game feature.

Conceptualization	Thinks beyond immediate goals to ensure long-term success.	A Raid Leader organizes a schedule that prepares the team for end-game content.	Aligns production schedules to support the game's overall vision.
Foresight	Anticipates challenges and prepares accordingly.	A Squad Leader anticipates an opponent's tactics and preps the team with counter strategies.	Plans ahead for potential delays in content delivery and resource allocation.
Stewardship	Takes responsibility for the team's success and well-being.	A Raid Leader fairly distributes loot and ensures every role gets the support they need.	Ensures fair workload distribution across teams to avoid burnout.
Commitment to Growth	Encourages learning and development within the team.	A Squad Leader creates drills to improve teamwork and tactical execution.	Provides training opportunities and career development pathways for the team.
Building Community	Fosters meaningful connections and collaboration.	A Raid Leader arranges casual game nights or meetups to solidify team camaraderie.	Organizes cross disciplinary meetings to strengthen team synergy.

While I first learned about servant leadership early on in my video game production career, I did not understand the full scope of its principles. At first, it seemed straightforward: to be a servant leader, you must serve your team. I, like many others, took this too literally and assumed it meant performing minor tasks for the team, like bringing coffee, cleaning up after them, or taking notes during meetings. I would go above and beyond in making sure my team's needs were met so that they would have no distractions, which was great, but I was missing something. If you look at the 10 pillars above, none of them focus on simply serving or acting as a servant.

The key element of this entire approach is literally in the name: Leadership.

Servant leadership is about guiding a team toward a larger purpose that unites everyone. It was Leo's intention to create a shared vision with his travelers. He wasn't serving the team; he was serving the journey across the desert.

Much of Greenleaf's early work applied to college institutions and the educational system, but his learnings transcend that industry. In another essay, he discusses dreams and ideas. We can adapt that to the way that a shared vision connects to the mentality of how to serve.

From Robert K. Greenleaf's essay, *New Dreams Are Needed*:

> *"It is not 'I,' the ultimate leader, that is moving this institution to greatness; it is the dream, the great idea. 'I' am subordinate to the idea; 'I' am servant of the idea along with everyone else who is involved in the effort."*[6]

When you consider the principles of servant leadership as a whole, you should focus on serving the shared vision, not serving just the people. In the video game industry, I've seen how misunderstandings about servant leadership can still create problems.

Especially because I write this as a male in an industry that remains heavily male-dominated.

When women and people of other identities embrace servant leadership, stereotypes about servitude can sometimes lead to unfair treatment and a lack of recognition. I've had several

---

6   Greenleaf, R. K. (2016). The Power of Servant Leadership. Brilliance Publishing.

conversations with my mentors and bosses, who were women, with very strong and valid feelings on the topic of servant leadership. They felt like their work wasn't valued because they were expected to practice servant leadership, but it had been twisted into something that pushed old-school, toxic expectations onto women and minorities. Some of those outdated ideas still suggest that women or minorities shouldn't be in leadership and are only suited for the "small" tasks, things like cleaning up, grabbing snacks, or taking notes for meetings. It ends up feeding into this weird servant dynamic and creates a top-down structure that shouldn't be there in the first place. I want to be very clear. This is not the servant leadership that I am talking about.

My goal is to clarify the servant leader's message so that it is not understood through those toxic behaviors. When applied correctly with all the principles embraced and practiced, servant leadership strengthens teams and transforms them into a group that continuously supports one another.

For example, a key function of the producer when leading and managing teams is to take meeting notes for the team so there is a record of the action items and decisions that were discussed. The stereotype that this is equivalent to being like a secretary is both sexist and inaccurate, but it still persists.

To break that mold, I do not focus on the act of taking notes. Instead, I try to take on the mindset of a Support character in *League of Legends*. I ask myself what my teammates need in this meeting, and who requires the most help.

For example, does Nick, the programmer, need detailed notes, or would a bullet-point list of action items be more useful?

The goal is not just to summarize key actions from the meeting but to present them in a way that Nick finds valuable. In return, you need to make sure Nick understands that this is not about servitude but a tool I use to become a force multiplier. Just like the *League of Legends* story, when we explain and find out how to help each other, our actions are in servitude to the greater shared vision.

However, as a video game producer, I have been on teams where I applied this strategy, but no one even read my notes.

I realized that it was not because note-taking was not valuable; it just was not valuable for that particular team. Some teams prefer discussing takeaways directly instead of reading documentation. In that situation, rather than insisting on an unused system, I shift my focus. I ask myself what is actually valuable in the meeting and help steer the team toward those results.

This concept extends beyond note-taking, but it's a good place to start. Once you embrace servant leadership principles that align with your team's shared vision, you may notice greater appreciation from your team as you add value for them. With more consistency and being able to perform the same results, appreciation turns into trust. Trust has the ability to reward you with something that should not be taken lightly, either. In the end, you'll earn the ultimate reward, a double-edged sword called **"Power."**

TYPES OF POWER & INFLUENCE

Baldur's Gate 3 is a game in which every choice has consequences. Based on the tabletop classic *Dungeons & Dragons*, it brings the same freedom of decision-making and fluid storytelling as its predecessor. Instead of rolling real dice, *Baldur's Gate* determines outcomes through your character's stats, skills, and luck. Whether it is through charm, brute force, or deception, your words can alter the course of events.

If you are a fan of the game, take the following example as fan fiction, as this scene doesn't actually happen.

Imagine you are standing before Dror Ragzlin, the self-proclaimed goblin king, inside the ruined temple that serves as his war camp. The scent of roasted meat and stale blood hangs thick in the air. Goblins lounge across the room, watching and whispering among themselves. The Absolute's symbol is painted across the stone walls, a subtle reminder of its influence on the king.

Dror Ragzlin slouches in his throne, with his scarred arms draped over the armrests. His eyes hold amusement, but there is curiosity in them as well.

"You have nerve, waltzing in here like you own the place," he rumbles, his voice thick with arrogance. His grip tightens on the hilt of his weapon. "Tell me, why shouldn't I have my boys gut you right now?"

You have several ways to respond. A strong approach may earn his respect; a clever one may turn the situation in your favor, or a mistake could end in an all-out battle.

Let's look at our options for a response to him:

1. **[Use Intimidation] "I have killed bigger things than you today. Try me, and I'll make an example out of you."** *(Requires an Intimidation Check - success makes Dror Ragzlin hesitate, failure turns the room hostile.)*

2. **[Use Persuasion] "You need someone with my skills. I can get things done that your goblins never could."** *(Requires a Persuasion Check - success may earn you favor, failure makes him laugh in your face.)*

3. **[Use Deception] "The Absolute sent me. I carry her will, and I doubt she'd be pleased if you got in my way."** *(Requires a Deception Check - if you convince him, you might gain influence over the cultists. If you fail, he sees through the lie and calls for*

your execution.)

4. **[Attack] (Draw your weapon and strike first.)**
   (Initiates combat immediately. Hope you're ready for a fight.)

Choosing option #4 is never that bad as an option. Otherwise, however you choose to respond, your words will carry weight. What you say and how you say it do shape the story. Every decision affects the outcome, and the way you approach a situation determines the result. Perhaps an intimidated Dror Ragzlin will let you travel through his domain, only to send assassins after you. Or, his fear of the Absolute might prompt him to offer you a special quest that is inaccessible elsewhere in the game. There are no wrong answers, only consequences.

In the real world, choices are not determined by dice rolls or randomly generated numbers. Convincing others to follow your lead requires an understanding of the consequences of your approach, the patience to earn credibility, and an understanding of how others may manipulate things. People, especially strangers, do not instantly trust each other. Some methods of earning trust take time and effort; others use force to speed up the process.

When we talk about **power in leadership**, *it's the ability to influence people, resources, and events to achieve goals.* There are three types of power I want to discuss, but only one strengthens a team, unites people, and creates long-term success. Power is like a double-edged sword. It can be used to inspire and guide, or it can be wielded recklessly, creating division. It must be handled with respect.

When a leader earns the trust of their team, they gain the ability to influence its direction, which is a form of power. A leader's actions set the example, and the team hopefully mimics those behaviors in order to achieve project success. A well-respected leader does not rely solely on the authority of their position or title. Their power comes from the trust and willingness of the people who follow them.

I have witnessed several different leadership styles first-hand in *Guild Wars 2*. *Guild Wars 2* is an MMORPG that has some of the best big, open-world PvP battles. Large groups of players formed elite guilds to fight in these battles. Each guild leader used power in their own way, and the results varied. Some built strong, dedicated teams, while others created instability through poor leadership. Understanding these experiences provides insight into what makes power a force for growth or destruction.

The three types of power that we will be looking at are:

1. **Coercive power**

2. **Manipulative power**

3. **Persuasive power**

Let's start with the first, the most stereotypical type of power, used by most villains in video games and fantasy stories.

Coercive power *involves using punishment or threats to ensure team members follow rules and meet objectives.* It may seem effective in the short term, as it creates immediate obedience and structure, but it comes at the expense of trust and morale.

Over time, coercion weakens a team rather than strengthening it. People do not follow the leader out of respect or because they believe in the vision. They follow because they are afraid of the consequences if they do not. This approach creates an environment of resentment and disengagement. When fear is the driving force, people do the bare minimum to avoid punishment rather than pushing themselves to achieve something greater.

Coercive power is unsustainable. It does not build loyalty, nor does it inspire people to work together. The moment fear fades or the leader loses control, this type of power collapses.

In the *Guild Wars 2* community, I joined a highly active guild focused on world-versus-world raiding. This guild leader took charge on the front lines, actively leading every engagement.

Large-scale fights in *Guild Wars 2* revolve around guilds moving as a single coordinated group, often called a "blob." In this playstyle, everyone stays tightly packed instead of spreading out. The idea was simple. Our leader formed us into a giant ball of players, a blob. They dictated every movement, calling for the entire group to shift left, right, or reposition based on the other enemy player's position. With enough coordination, the blob could overwhelm scattered opponents through sheer force and organization. These battles required constant communication from the Guild Leader, and we had to be in voice tools like Discord or TeamSpeak to stay in sync.

This Guild Leader was widely regarded as the best on the server, and for good reason. Our guild excelled on the server's PvP battlegrounds, winning more engagements than any other group because of his battle-leadership. When we were in action, we looked like a perfectly synchronized machine, every member in their exact position, moving together. It was the kind of teamwork that looked almost magical, as if we shared a collective mind. From the outside, it was hard not to be impressed.

Inside the guild, though, the reality was far less enchanting. The leader ruled through undiplomatic approaches, relying on coercive power to keep everyone in line. Showing up late meant you wouldn't get to play, regardless of your real-world responsibilities. A misstep on one of his call-outs, like turning right when told to go left, could result in both your in-game death and a public shaming. You could expect he would make fun of you in front of everyone in the call just to embarrass you.

This method has some direct results and after-effects. The fear of punishment generally kept everyone in line. We had a culture of one-sided communication in which orders were followed without question. Mistakes were rare because the consequences were immediate and hurtful, which no one wanted to experience.

For a time, it worked. But the constant pressure made the game feel more like a job. What started as something people enjoyed became a source of stress. Players gradually drifted away, looking for communities where they could play without the fear of failure looming over them. While coercive power can deliver results quickly and effectively in a game, I consider the cost to be far too high. Fun should always be the priority when you play a game. While I enjoyed winning, I eventually drifted away from that particular guild to find a better culture.

The second type of power works behind the scenes, influencing people without them realizing it. Instead of using direct threats, manipulative leaders control situations by twisting facts or withholding key information. This approach allows them to guide outcomes while keeping their true intentions hidden.

Over time, manipulation damages relationships and creates uncertainty. People may follow along without question at first, but once they realize they have been misled, the trust begins to erode. The workplace or team environment becomes tense as members hesitate to share ideas or rely on leadership.

Manipulative Power *often involves presenting knowingly false, incomplete, or distorted reasoning to achieve a specific outcome. It may use deception, hidden agendas, or emotional exploitation to sway others.*

In a different *Guild Wars 2* guild, I saw an example of a manipulative leader. He kept convincing members to repeatedly run a certain dungeon by promising valuable rewards. He framed it as a way for everyone to gather materials for gear upgrades. What he left out was his personal agenda. The dungeon contained a rare item he needed for his legendary weapon. For his specific role, this was the most powerful weapon in the game. The rest of the group kept running it, thinking they were working toward a shared goal. In reality, he was the only one who truly benefited.

Once he secured the item he wanted, his deception grew. Rather than keeping his promise to help others with their gear, he shifted focus to a different rare item, claiming it was now essential for the guild's success. The group, unaware of his changing motives, kept running dungeons under the assumption they were working toward a shared goal. Each time he got what he wanted, he moved on, leaving the team empty-handed and frustrated.

Instead of strengthening teamwork, this kind of manipulation erodes trust and weakens the group from within. By pretending his personal goals were for the group's benefit, he turned what should have been a shared effort into a selfish pursuit. When the truth eventually came out, it was impossible to repair the damage. Players left, relationships soured, and what had once been a cohesive guild fell apart.

Manipulative power is deceptive in nature, concealing itself under the pretense of unity. It tricks people into believing they're part of something bigger, only to reveal that they were being used for someone else's gain. In games, as in life, this betrayal stings deeply and often leaves lasting scars. Trust, once lost, rarely returns.

The third power type is the only other option available to leaders when they are wielding power within their teams.

Persuasive Power *is rooted in genuine reasoning, truth, and mutual understanding. It is based on presenting information, arguments, or ideas that are contextualized with the facts at hand.* The intent is to empower others to make informed decisions with transparent reasoning. It embodies the principles of servant leadership, enabling leaders to guide their teams without relying on authority or deceit, but on trust.

I saw this play out during another *Guild Wars 2* experience. Our raid group wanted to gather crafting materials and gold for our guild bank. The goal was to make both repairs and food free for everyone in our guild. Instead of every player having to farm materials or spend gold individually, members could volunteer to make the food from the materials donated. This would save everyone time and effort in the long run. Success depended on every member contributing materials or gold to the guild's bank, where the leader would have full control. Without a clear understanding of how this should work, there was a risk people would abuse this; our leader understood this better than anyone.

Before we began, he gathered the group and explained the entire plan in detail. He did not just tell us what to do. He broke down the reasoning behind each step. "I want you all to understand why this matters," he said. "Repairs and food cost gold, and crafting takes time. If we all gather efficiently and contribute, our guild crafters will handle the work for us. That means no one has to worry about farming materials alone or spending extra gold on supplies. Everyone benefits, and we keep our focus where it matters." He made it clear that his role was not to issue blind orders but to guide the team toward a shared goal. Understanding the rationale behind the plan was key to making it work.

After presenting the plan, he paused and asked if anyone had questions or concerns. He encouraged even the quieter players to speak up and welcomed their input. Some raised concerns about emergency scenarios where they might need to access the guild bank when the leader was not online. Instead of brushing them aside, he addressed each point thoughtfully and revised the plan where it made sense. We all agreed on what items should be freely taken amongst the members and that they should have access to them.

It wasn't long before the guild bank was fully stocked. Every player now had access to free repairs and food.

True persuasion comes from building trust and alignment through open dialogue and rational responses. This leader created a safe space in which everyone could understand and agree on the vision. Persuasive power doesn't rely on tricks or commands. It thrives on clarity and the shared confidence of a team working toward clear and rational goals.

If you use this type of persuasion while communicating with your team, you are already developing an important leadership skill. Persuasion allows you to shape discussions, gain support, and guide decisions by simply finding agreement amongst your team. When you communicate persuasively, you set the tone for how decisions are made. Your team observes how you approach situations, and over time, that influence spreads. It encourages a culture where people pay attention to what works and adjust their own behavior based on what they see in leadership.

As we can see from the examples above, the servant leader's power comes from having influence. It's this influence over a team that keeps everyone together and working toward a clear vision. Influence helps a leader to open people's minds to new ideas and create change. It isn't always just reason and logic that drives persuasive powers. Often, this type of power comes from the leader's behavior and the way they exemplify the values that matter most. A leader who understands influence does not just use it for personal gain, but to rally their teams. They create an environment where the team understands the importance of working together.

To better understand persuasive power, let's take a closer look at influence. Robert Cialdini, a respected psychologist and author, introduced six principles for understanding influence in persuasion. I have shortened them for simplicity's sake and removed his sixth principle, which was scarcity, as it feels less central to servant leadership. Leaders who understand these principles can easily identify them in others who are trying to lead.

- **Reciprocity** - People naturally respond in kind when they receive support or generosity.

- **Commitment and Consistency** - Once people commit to a goal, they are more likely to follow.

- **Social Proof** - People look to others for cues on how to behave, especially in uncertain situations.

- **Authority** - Expertise and credibility inspire trust.

- **Liking** - People are more influenced by those they connect with and respect.

Each of these principles can be used as a tool to influence.

An observant leader will mix and match these options to find what works best for specific situations and teammates. I hope you can recognize the different types of influence you have already experienced in games and how familiar they can be. Listed below is another take on how the principles might be seen by a Squad Leader or Raid Leader that you can relate to.

Principle	Squad Leader	Raid Leader
Reciprocity	Shares ammo and health packs with teammates to keep everyone in the fight.	Provides potions and buffs before a tough encounter, ensuring the team is prepared.
Commitment & Consistency	Rallies the squad to stick to the mission plan even when under heavy fire.	Holds players accountable for not following orders and reinforces discipline through repetition.
Social Proof	Speaks calmly and confidently over comms, setting the tone for teamwork and focus.	Shows patience and composure during wipes, keeping the team focused on improvement.
Authority	Helps execute their own commands to consistently show what is possible.	Explains boss strategies clearly and concisely, gaining the team's trust in their leadership.
Liking	Checks in on teammates between fights to keep morale high through camaraderie.	Encourages and praises players for executing mechanics well, keeping the energy positive.

If we dive a little deeper into my favorite three, Authority, Liking, and Social Proof, I can share how they apply to a video game producer and how to use them together.

The key to influence as a producer isn't always about wielding it yourself. It's about knowing when to leverage it or find the right person on the team who already has it. Influence isn't a solo act; it's about knowing where to apply pressure and who can help you apply it effectively.

Authority *comes from expertise and credibility.*

It is possible to get this by title, but that is not really what I am getting at. Producers and in-game leaders should be earning their authority through servant leadership. The act of following those principles and being there for your team gives you an indirect title of leader, regardless of your actual title.

Also, as a producer, you may not always be the subject matter expert, but you can bring in those who are to partner with you. Let's say you need to align the team with the engineers on a technical feature. Instead of explaining the problem yourself, you could bring in the senior developer who wrote the code to walk the team through the challenge. The authority, in this case, doesn't come from you. It comes from that developer's deep understanding. Recognizing who holds authority in different areas and using it effectively ensures that solutions are well-founded and respected.

Social Proof *is the principle that people look to the behaviors and norms of others, especially in uncertain situations, to guide their own decisions.*

On a video game team, these are often the unwritten rules, things like *"we don't crunch"* or *"our weekends are sacred."*

A producer can use Social Proof to remind the team of these values when decisions start to drift. If someone suggests extending work hours to hit a milestone, a well-placed, *"That's not how we do things here,"* can be powerful in steering the conversation back toward sustainable work habits. It's about reinforcing what has already been agreed upon as the team's cultural standard. By doing so, the team will respect you and know that you are looking out for them.

Liking is one of the most underrated tools in a producer's arsenal. *People are more likely to collaborate and follow the lead of someone they like and trust.*

This means investing in genuine relationships with your teammates. Creating friendships is nice, but not everyone needs to be your friend. There should be a professional expectation that you are a friendly, approachable person who is looking out for everyone's best interests. So, it requires being present for your teammates, listening to their concerns, and offering support that goes beyond the work itself. When trust and camaraderie are established, alignment does not need to be forced. It happens naturally because people want to work with you.

Throughout my career as a video game producer, I have been so focused on those three types of influence that they are core to my beliefs about how to work with others. For example, when I join a new team, the first thing I do is get to know my teammates. This involves literally reaching out to introduce yourself and trying to carve out some time to actually sit down and talk with them. If you are in a work-from-home environment, that just means setting up a Zoom or Discord video chat and chatting for 30 minutes a week in a one-on-one. Or even better, taking some time to play some video games together.

Once I start building bonds and relationships with my teammates, I try to be as consistent as possible in my actions. If you make mistakes, it's important to own up to them, but unfortunately, that doesn't give you a proven track record, which can be a negative. I continue to make a name for myself by letting my work speak for itself and by getting teams aligned in a friendly, approachable way toward a shared goal. Authority isn't something that is always granted just by having a title, but something that needs to be earned. If I have earned my team's respect, then that means I can speak on their behalf because they trust me to do so.

Hopefully, these examples show the power of using persuasion to make change as a leader. I did not include the toolset of how to use coercion to produce authority-driven alignment because it does not belong in my frameworks. That method undermines trust and creates resistance rather than cooperation. Influence, when used correctly, fosters a culture where teams engage willingly because of the positive nature of the principles. Producers who lead by example are demonstrating how others should behave. This reinforces a cycle in which strong leadership continues to grow within the team through imitation. That is why it's extremely important not to introduce negative influence to the team's toolbox of leadership values.

Every producer will develop their own approach to influence. These principles are not meant to be used in isolation. The most effective leaders mix and match them, adjusting based on the situation. Influence becomes the strongest tool when combined with persuasion, ensuring people feel heard, motivated, and invested in the team's success. What style fits you and do you foresee if you are going to have to make any changes later in the future?

FORESIGHT, WISDOM, AND INTUITION OH MY!

Why do some leaders (and, in our case, gamers) seem to anticipate problems before they happen, almost as if they can see the future? It's not luck, although it often appears to be. Rather, it is one of the core principles of servant leadership: Foresight. Before I give you my definition of this term, let's see what the professionals have to say. Larry C. Spears, the Executive Director of The Greenleaf Center for Servant-Leadership since 1990, published his definition of Foresight in the journal, "Character and Servant Leadership: Ten Characteristics of Effective, Caring Leaders."

"One knows foresight when one experiences it. Foresight is a characteristic that enables the servant leader to understand the lessons from the past, the realities of the present, and the likely consequences of a decision for the future. It is also deeply rooted within the intuitive mind."[7] - Larry C. Spears

Foresight is a critical element in game design to keep players engaged and to encourage them to recognize patterns. One particular video game genre captures this idea perfectly. Games like **Rogue** (1980) introduced permadeath, which is also why the "rogue" genre was named after it. Permadeath forces players to plan every move carefully or risk losing everything and starting over. Unlike traditional platformer games, *Rogue* did not allow brute-force strategies. Survival meant thinking ahead, learning from mistakes, and making better choices next time.

Roguelike and **roguelite** are terms used to describe subgenres of games that draw inspiration from *Rogue*. Both feature procedurally generated levels and permadeath, but they differ in key aspects. Roguelike games aim to closely emulate the original *Rogue* experience. They typically feature turn-based, grid-based movement, and when a player dies, they lose all progress and start each new game from scratch. This design emphasizes strategic planning and adaptability, as each playthrough presents unique challenges.

Roguelite games, while incorporating elements from *Rogue*, offer a more forgiving experience. They often include meta-progression, allowing players to unlock abilities, items, or upgrades that persist between runs. This means that, even after a character's death, some form of progress remains, potentially making future attempts easier.

One of the best modern examples of the roguelite gameplay loop is *Hades* (2020) by Supergiant Games. You play as Zagreus, son

---

7   Spears, L. C. (1995). *Reflections on Leadership: How Robert K. Greenleaf's theory of servant-leadership influenced today's top management thinkers*. New York: John Wiley & Sons.

of Hades, and you are trying to escape the underworld. Every time you die, you're sent back to the House of Hades to start over, but your progress isn't erased. You keep the resources you collected, and they help you unlock new abilities once you return home, making you stronger each playthrough.

At first, enemies seem overwhelming, and bosses feel impossible to defeat because of your lower-skilled abilities. But as you repeat each run, you start to recognize patterns. You notice how an enemy pauses before attacking or that certain weapons work better in different situations. Each attempt teaches you something new. Even if you don't clear the underworld, you still gain permanent upgrades that improve your health, attack damage, and/or speed.

This is how *Hades* teaches foresight. The more you play, the more you understand what's ahead. You stop reacting to disruptions and start preparing for them. The same rules apply outside of games.

What is **foresight**? *It's the ability to predict or anticipate what will be needed in the future.*

However, foresight doesn't act alone. It works alongside **intuition** and **wisdom** to create effective decision-making.

- **Intuition** *is that gut feeling, the immediate insight that kicks in before conscious reasoning.* It's how you instinctively dodge an enemy attack before even fully processing the danger.

- **Wisdom** *allows you to apply past lessons effectively, refining your approach with each experience.*

Gamers who play roguelites are routinely practicing both of these skills. It's a learned ability that improves with practice.

When we play video games, intuition and wisdom are constantly at work. We start by understanding how the game world operates, by observing how elements behave, and trying to find patterns.

Sometimes enemies spawn based on location, sometimes on timers, and sometimes in response to player actions. These patterns reveal visual and audio cues, such as a distant roar signaling an approaching threat or a flickering light hinting at an interactive object.

Over time, we come to recognize these signals and anticipate what's coming next, allowing us to make strategic choices before a challenge fully presents itself. This sparks our intuition. With every attempt, our wisdom grows as we refine the ways we approach challenges, adjust our strategies, and adapt to unexpected changes.

Next time you play, focus on the cues the game gives you. Notice how sound effects or visual markers trigger incoming events. Ask yourself if it was intuition or wisdom that was actively contributing to your foresight.

In video game production, foresight is essential when it comes to keeping projects on track. A producer's foresight is critical to preventing delays and ensuring a team's shared vision stays on course. When a producer makes a decision about timelines or resources, they do so with any potential problems identified and solutions accounted for. If they see a roadblock coming, they can set team expectations before it slows everything down.

This is using foresight to identify **risks**, *the possibility of an event that could impact a project's objectives.* Producers think ahead about what the team will need, or might need, even if the team isn't thinking about it yet. They do this to mitigate potential risks from happening. That might mean identifying when a missed deliverable date might occur because the team is running into other unforeseen problems. We can therefore escalate this problem to the right people in order to avoid a bigger problem in the future.

Foresight in video game production also means recognizing patterns. Producers build deep bonds with their teams and learn how different people respond to challenges. Every team has its own way of handling problems, and paying attention to your team's human cues allows for your wisdom and intuition to help see it before it happens.

For example, if a video game artist avoids character animation work whenever possible, that's a pattern worth noticing. Instead of waiting for frustration to set in, a producer can anticipate when new animation tasks are coming and check in with the artist beforehand. They might offer extra time, shift priorities, or ask another teammate for help. This kind of foresight doesn't just keep production moving; it helps maintain trust.

This also applies to communication and information sharing. Some teams prefer direct and to-the-point discussions, while others need more context before making decisions. Certain people respond better to casual check-ins, while others prefer formal updates. A producer who recognizes these cultural patterns can adjust their approach to fit what works best.

Foresight also helps reduce unnecessary stress. If a team struggles with presenting their work, a producer can prepare them in advance to ease that pressure. They might arrange a smaller internal review before a major presentation or offer guidance on how to structure their updates. Instead of letting these moments create disruption, the producer needs the wisdom to recognize the pattern and the intuition to know it might be a problem.

This ability to anticipate and adjust is far more effective than being in the dark and relying on reactive leadership. Just as players in a roguelite learn from past runs to reach further with each attempt, great producers apply lessons from past projects to create smoother, more effective production cycles.

Leadership in game production mirrors a great roguelite run. The challenges are unpredictable, the stakes are high, and progress depends on adaptation and learning from past mistakes.

Below is a simplified breakdown of how foresight, intuition, and wisdom function in both roguelikes and game production:

Concept	Example from Roguelikes	Video Game Production
Foresight is sharpened by intuition and wisdom.	Learning to anticipate enemy spawn points based on level progression.	Ensuring the QA team has enough time to test a new feature and find additional bugs.
Intuition and pattern recognition.	Dodging an enemy attack instinctively after seeing similar behavior.	Noticing that your team doesn't like to be surprised by last minute requests.
Wisdom helps not to repeat mistakes.	Dodging an enemy attack because you remembered the last time it killed you.	Not to launch an update on a Friday night, if it fails, it ruins the weekend.

Foresight, intuition, and wisdom don't just help players progress through a roguelike. They define how great producers navigate the unpredictable terrain of game development. Foresight alone isn't enough to solve all problems, though it does help you to see and mitigate risks or potential roadblocks. True leadership extends beyond simply identifying the problem and aims to eliminate risks by building repeatable, consistent systems that empower teams to work efficiently and adapt to evolving challenges.

A producer's ability to anticipate problems feeds directly into how they design and optimize human systems. Just as a roguelite player refines their strategy with each attempt, a producer refines the human systems their team relies on, ensuring long-term success. These systems evolve with the team, scaling to meet their needs while keeping production aligned with the shared vision.

Leadership is understanding the vision and changing that to a shared vision with others. It's about having the ability to use types of power and influence around people who trust and rely on you to use them appropriately. They want you to use foresight to see future risks and find ways to mitigate them before they hit the team. If we agree that you already have experience in these abilities because of your video game experiences, then let's talk about how we use them when building systems with others.

HUMAN SYSTEM BUILDING

In 2006, my team and I were competing in a *Counter-Strike: Source* LAN tournament in Tracy, California, and we had made it to the final round.

The room was packed on both sides with spectators watching us compete. However, the roar of the crowd was more noticeable for the opposing team's star player, Nova. He had been winning rounds back to back, bringing his team to the final round, only seconds away from victory. I wasn't worried, though, as my team still had the advantage in the final fight. The rest of his team had been eliminated, but we still had two alive: Ryan and me. The map's name was Nuke, and Nova had just planted (placed the objective) in the facility's upper bomb location. Nova had full control of the situation, with multiple angles to defend from. Ryan and I were in the first-floor lobby, waiting just outside the bomb site. Our only option was to move in and defuse the bomb before time ran out, or it would detonate, giving Nova the win in the final round.

Ryan called it first. "Let's go through the hut to retake the site."

Hut was our shorthand for the small connector leading into the warehouse. I yelled back, "I'll throw two flashes. I'll clear the mini connector and vents. You cover rafters."

"Got it," Ryan replied.

I threw both flashbangs, bouncing them off the hut wall at the correct angle so they would land safely in the warehouse without blinding us. The flashbangs popped around the corner. No time to hesitate.

"Go! Go! Go!" we yelled together.

I was the entry fragger. First through the door. First to take the risk. The downside? He knew we were coming.

I moved fast, sweeping my crosshairs across the rafters. There was no sign of him.

Ryan called from behind, "Connector clear!"

I checked the bombsite, scanning every inch. No movement. He had either left the building or repositioned to the top of the ladder, which led to the rafters we called Heaven.

We had 20 seconds left.

I yelled, "Ryan, I'm going for the defuse. Cover me!"

Ryan repositioned himself near the crates beside the bomb. I crouched and tapped the defuse button. The game made the telltale clicking sound, a signal that every player hears.

A shot cracked from above.

"Rafters!" Ryan shouted, but it was too late. A single sniper round hit him, dropping him instantly. The crowd erupted as Nova let out a victorious yell.

Ryan was dead. Now it was Nova versus me.

I stopped defusing instantly and snap-aimed to the position from which Nova fired. If I looked down again to defuse, Nova would peek and finish me. But if he waited, the bomb would detonate, and he would still win. He now had the advantage. I had the bombs tick as a consistent reminder that time was also against me.

I steadied my aim, crosshairs still locked on the rafters' corner where he fired from last. I needed him to move first. But he was too smart to let that happen.

I decided to risk it. I looked down at the bomb, pretending I was going back for the defuse to lure him out. The moment I hit the defuse key, the audio cue played, and as predictable as Nova is, he peeked. He thought he could land another shot before I had a chance to react.

But I was already moving. A flick of the wrist and a squeeze of the trigger is all it took.

Boom headshot.

I exhaled, not realizing I'd been holding my breath. "Nova, that was close!" I yelled across the LAN center's room, before defusing the bomb for real to win the round within the time limit.

The match was ours. The crowd on our side erupted. The win felt electric, but it wasn't just about this final moment. It was the journey and all the practice and work leading up to it. A giant weight was lifted from my shoulders.

We had spent hours practicing our *Counter-Strike* site-clearing drills, burning them into muscle memory. We had practiced over and over, covering different situations, imagining where opponents could be, and planning how to retake the site together. We knew how to move as a single unit each time, how to call out locations in our own shorthand, and how to react without hesitation. It's not just that we knew the strategy; we drilled it into our brains and muscle memory through repetition, so we knew it worked under pressure. The fake defuse wasn't a last-minute gamble. It was something we had rehearsed. A player like Nova wouldn't be able to ignore it. We knew he would react. He had been aggressive the whole match.

That is the beauty of a reliable system. When the pressure is at its peak and the stakes are high, you don't rely on luck. You rely on the system.

Human Systems Building *is the producer's craft of designing and implementing systems that enable teams to succeed consistently and repeatedly.*

As producers, we have access to pre-designed, reliable, and consistent systems such as Agile and Scrum. We will discuss these in more detail in the next sections. However, these off-the-shelf systems rarely fit perfectly because our team members and projects are often unique, so fitting them into such systems can feel like putting a square peg in a round hole.

As human systems builders, producers must first understand how these frameworks might work with their specific teams.

For example, a small indie team might be successful with simple tools like sticky notes and quick daily check-ins, while a large AAA studio will need structured workflows, dedicated roles and assignments, and task-tracking software like *Jira*.

Some teams prefer short development cycles with frequent playtests, while others work better with longer planning phases before making changes. A producer's effectiveness depends on recognizing what helps a team function efficiently without forcing them into rigid processes that don't fit.

Let's talk about how we, as video game producers, can find the right system for a specific team. It doesn't matter how big or small the team is if you can embrace this concept. This brings me to my favorite non-video game analogy, which I use with my junior producers. I find this one helpful for understanding what systems you should pair with a team.

I call it "The Hammer and the Screws."

Imagine you're assigned to a team to create a system or process that acts as a force multiplier for the team. The gimmick is that you are all different types of tools. In this scenario, the team members are literal "Screws," an advanced fastening tool capable of holding wood together more securely due to its spiral design, which grips into the material. They work best with a "Screwdriver," a specialized tool that fits into the tip of the screw to twist the screw into wood.

You, however, are "The Hammer," a tool designed for vertical smashing, best suited for nails. Nails are long cylinders that can be driven into two pieces of wood to hold them together. Screws and nails each have their tradeoffs: screws create a stronger, more stable hold, but they require more time and effort to install. Nails, while faster to work with, are less reliable for holding things together under strain.

What should you do as the hammer in this situation if you want to work well with that team of screws? You have a few options:

1. As "The Hammer," should you change into a "Screwdriver" to be compatible with the team?

2. Should the team adapt to you and switch from "Screws"

to "Nails," for faster installation?

3. Or should neither change, so we use the hammer to just smash the screws into the wood?

The answer isn't about forcing one side to change. A hammer might be powerful, but if the job requires screws, brute force isn't the solution. The best approach is to find the right tool for the job. In a producer's case, that means finding the right system for the team.

This analogy underscores the importance of taking the time to use foresight on how a system might work with your team rather than forcing a pre-designed system. The ability to analyze team dynamics is central to effective human system design. A great producer doesn't just bring a toolbox. They know when to swap tools, adjust techniques, and step back. The right system allows the team to function at its best. The difference between the two systems could be the deciding factor between a slow team and an unstoppable one.

Video game producers must evaluate their team members' expertise levels and workload capacity in order to create systems and workflows that maximize efficiency.

For example, if a junior developer is assigned a task, they may need more time to learn the tools, understand best practices, or seek guidance from more experienced teammates. Their system should account for ramp-up time, mentorship, and structured feedback. A senior developer, on the other hand, will need other things. They already have the knowledge and experience to execute quickly. Their system should focus on autonomy, removing blockers, and ensuring they aren't bogged down by unnecessary oversight.

If both engineers are treated the same, the system will fail them in different ways. The junior will struggle without enough support, and the senior will feel slowed down and underutilized. A well-designed system doesn't just track work. It considers the people using it and adapts to their needs.

Once a system is determined, it's critical to set an example for working within it. In *Counter-Strike,* we would practice over and over again so that everyone on the team fully understood their roles. The saying, "Lead by example," means you must follow your own rules to help others understand what success looks like. By consistently modeling the correct behavior for your systems, you and your team set the standards. Once the standards are set, the new team members who join will also start to mimic this behavior in your system; it becomes the standard by which all members, new or old, conduct themselves.

In this first section of the book, it is vital to understand that the first part of being a producer is leading. Leading is earning the trust of your team and aligning them under a shared vision. If you can not find the right way to influence others, use types of power that resonate with the team, or have the foresight to prevent mistakes, it will be hard for people to trust your system.

When I played with my friends in *Counter-Strike,* we earned each other's trust and knew how we were going to move and think. When we set the standards, we also took the time to get to know each other. Just like in the hammer and screws story, not every system worked with my team right out of the gate. We had to adjust our systems and processes to fit us. It didn't matter what worked for other people; we did it our way.

Working on game development teams, the same bonds can be formed with your other team members. You can understand how they will operate and communicate with others. With these kinds of strong relationships, it's easier to get feedback on the systems you are trying to implement. It's important to know that no system is going to work just because you created it.

So where do we begin? Regardless of the system and the human factors, there is going to be a task list of work to handle. This is where every taskmaster starts. You need the ability to read and write the steps your teams will need to follow. In video games, these might be missions or quests, but in the video game development world, or in any industry really, these are called tasks. We are going to talk about the second part of being a producer: learning to manage. Let's start with what it means to be a taskmaster for your team.

PRODUCTION TASKMASTERS

"Hey! Listen!"

If you have never had the honor of playing *The Legend of Zelda: Ocarina of Time*, you are missing out on one of the most iconic shouts from the era of Nintendo 64 games.

In this game, you play as the main character, Link, a warrior on a quest to save the land. Alongside him is Navi, a fairy companion sent by the Great Deku Tree that helps guide you on your journey. She iconically says, "Hey! Listen!" every time she needs to get your attention.

As a player in the game, you grow to appreciate the intrusive and high-pitched "Hey! Listen!" The first time it happens, it does a great job of teaching wisdom, so you know that it will probably be important later on when she does it as well. These types of relationships appear in many video games. A hero often has someone supporting them, making sure they stay focused and helping them complete objectives.

Here are just a few of my favorite examples:

Halo features Master Chief and Cortana's partnership. The latter is an advanced AI that provides mission updates and deeper context to the narrative.

The Last of Us follows Joel and Ellie, and their connection strengthens as they rely on one another for survival, which, in turn, guides the player through the game.

In *Ratchet & Clank*, Ratchet is paired with Clank, a robotic companion who both offers strategic assistance and can help you get around the levels more easily.

Game designers include these companions for many reasons. They reinforce the story, ensure players stay on track, and offer extra information in a way that feels natural.

Video Game Studios like to have producers on the team for the same reason: to help the team stay on track and ensure everyone understands the context or vision for why we are doing those tasks.

You could say they hire us to be everyone's personal Navi.

To be a good video game producer, you must embrace task tracking for the team. A **Production Taskmaster** *tracks work and ensures the right amount is being done at the right time.*

It's surprising how many taskmaster-related systems we rely on without even realizing it. Have you ever used a player guide to beat a difficult boss? Or followed a quest log to keep track of objectives? Guides like these have been part of gaming culture for decades. In the 1980s and 90s, *Nintendo Power* wasn't just a magazine. It was a secret lifeline for players trying to figure out where to find the best items or how to unlock hidden content in their favorite games.

Today, digital resources have taken over. Websites like GameFAQs, IGN, and Polygon break down every aspect of a game, helping players master mechanics and find hidden details with easy-to-read guides. Online communities, from Reddit to Discord, provide real-time discussion where players trade strategies and socialize.

Streamers and content creators have also taken up the mantle of guide-making. They create in-depth tutorials for games like your favorite MMOs, showing exactly where to go and who to fight in order to level. If we were making a guide, we would try to break down the key information the player needs to know. It might look something like this:

- **Where to go** - Identifying the best locations for farming valuable resources or experience.

- **What to do there** - Sharing which monsters to fight and which monsters to avoid. Locating the areas that have the best spawns for materials to harvest.

- **When to move on** - Knowing when you have got all the valuable resources or have out-leveled the enemies.

- **What to keep or sell** - Sorting useful loot from items that are worth trading for gold or upgrades.

For example, a classic *World of Warcraft* farming guide might suggest:

"Go to Elwynn Forest and farm wolves for XP until level 10. Keep their hides and sell them at the auction house for gold. Once you reach level 10, move to Westfall, where the Defias Brotherhood enemies drop loot worth more gold and provide higher XP."

This is simple to understand and provides a straightforward method for what to do. Farming guides transform complex systems into clear steps, providing a reliable way to reach a goal.

A video game producer, acting as a production taskmaster, builds structured workflows that function similarly. They do not dictate creative decisions but collaborate with the team to refine systems and make them scalable.

While farming guides have fixed goals, game production constantly shifts. The questions remain familiar, but they must be adjusted for development and would look like this:

- **What needs to be done?** - Define the opportunity that we can make a feature for.

- **Why are we doing it?** - Identify the value this feature brings to the game.

- **Who needs to do it?** - Determine which team members are responsible for execution.

- **How long should each step take?** - Get realistic timelines for every stage of the process.

By organizing these elements, producers create structured task lists and workflows that guide the team toward completion. Let's give even more context to how this flow might work at a game studio. If a game development team is creating a new weapon, the production workflow might look like this:

Day1 (Monday)

Game Designer & Concept Artist: The designer works with the artist to define the weapon's purpose and mechanics. The concept artist sketches different versions before finalizing the visual reference.
Once the design is approved, it is handed off to the 3D artist.

Day 2 (Tuesday)

3D Artist: Models the weapon and applies textures based on the concept design.

Once the model is complete, it is sent to the animation, effects, and audio teams for further polishing.

Day 3 (Wednesday)

Animators: Create motion to ensure the weapon moves naturally in combat.

VFX Artist: Adds visual elements to enhance the weapons' look, such as glowing edges or impact sparks when they hit another object.

Audio Designer: Create sound effects for using the weapon, like the 'whooshing' sounds when swinging it.

Once animation, VFX, and sound are complete, everything is passed to engineering for integration.

Day 4 (Thursday)

Engineers: Bring the weapon into the game and ensure it functions properly, in line with the design document and the animations and VFX that should occur.

QA & Designers: Run tests to check functionality, look for technical issues, and adjust certain things like damage or speed outputs.

Day 5 (Friday)

Studio-Wide Playtest: The weapon is tested by the development team in real gameplay.

Feedback is gathered from multiple departments to identify any remaining issues or necessary adjustments.

Just as farming guides outline a step-by-step approach for players, production workflows create simple checklists, provide the order in which the work needs to be done, and establish who will be doing the work next. While this method is simple and makes a lot of sense, we can't always stick with just a checklist system because projects scale and teams expand, especially in AAA studios. This can lead to managing hundreds or even thousands of tasks for a single project. At that high a level, more structured workflows and guidelines are necessary to keep production moving forward.

Game studios use different frameworks to manage their development process. Some rely on structured planning, often called the Waterfall Method. Others use a more flexible iteration called Scrum. Picking which method to use brings us back to the Hammer and Screws analogy. It's up to you to understand all the options and weigh what is best for the team.

Let's look at these two methods more closely. The easiest one to start with is Waterfall.

A video game strategy or farming guide is extremely similar to the Waterfall process. They both represent a checklist that outlines a linear path to complete the work. The Waterfall methodology was first introduced by Dr. Winston W. Royce in a 1970 white paper titled "Managing the Development of Large Software Systems." Contrary to popular belief, Royce didn't present Waterfall as a perfect solution.

In fact, he explicitly pointed out its flaws, such as the difficulty of making changes later in the project lifecycle. Having said that, the methodology gained traction because it was intuitive and logical. Because it offers a clear, step-by-step approach to planning and task management, people gravitate toward Waterfall.

Waterfall follows a sequential order:

1. **Design and plan everything up front**

   - Every feature is outlined in detail.

   - The systems are mapped out to show how they interact.

2. **Execute according to the plan**

   - The development follows the design phase exactly as planned.

   - It must follow each step in a linear fashion.

3. **Test and verify the final product**

   - The goal is to ensure that everything works as expected.

   - The hope is that no major problems arise that require unexpected changes.

The biggest challenge with Waterfall is its linear flow in planning for the entire project. Once you reach later phases, making changes can be costly and difficult. If unforeseen issues arise during the testing and verification phase, adjustments may require reverting to the beginning, resulting in significant delays. While Waterfall works well in projects with clear, unchanging requirements (like construction or hardware manufacturing), video game development often requires more flexibility due to the iterative nature of design and the importance of player feedback.

The process makes sense when building something like a house. Let's say you want to build a one-story house. Start with the foundation, frame the structure, add the walls, and finish with the roof. Each step builds on the previous one in a logical, sequential order.

But what if you realize you want the house to be two stories while building the roof? It's not that easy to just say, "Let's add another floor!" with the snap of your fingers. We don't know whether the foundation being used or the frame supporting the house will be able to support the additional weight of adding a new floor.

In video game production, Waterfall can be applied as a linear path, but with the same faults. The project is broken into distinct phases, each building on the work of the previous one. For example:

1. **Design the Game:** Create detailed plans, concepts, and documentation outlining the game's features, mechanics, and scope.

2. **Program/Code the Game:** Begin developing the game based on the finalized design documents. This phase assumes the design is locked in.

3. **Make the Art:** Develop all visual and audio assets, including characters, environments, and soundtracks, often working within the parameters defined earlier.

4. **Test the Game:** Run through QA testing to identify bugs or ensure functionality matches the design specifications.

5. **Implement Feedback:** Incorporate feedback from testing, if possible.

Waterfall is useful when the work is known and will have minimal variations, like in an assembly line. I have seen it used very successfully by art and design teams because they approach their process in a linear way. For example, if an artist needs to make several types of swords in an upcoming RPG game, the process might be:

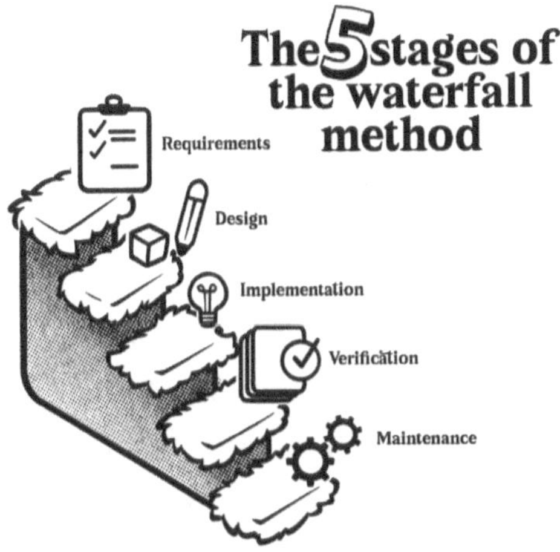

1. Design the sword on paper.

2. Finalize concept of the visual design.

3. Model the sword in 3D.

4. Add Visual Effects.

5. Add Audio.

6. Test.

These steps are not going to change order. You are not going to think about visual effects first and then design a sword. In this specific scenario of making a sword, each step is not very long or complicated, so the cost of going back to make a change is not a big deal. If we think about larger, more complex projects, like designing an entire game, we will want to discuss other frameworks for task management with an iterative approach, such as Scrum and Agile.

It's quite common for me to hear people using Scrum and Agile interchangeably, but they're not the same thing. Scrum is a process or system that predates Agile, while Agile is a broader methodology, or mindset, that supports various systems, including Scrum. Get it? No worries, I'll break it down further.

We are going to jump into the practical process of Scrum, but through the beneficial mindset of Agile.

Scrum was first implemented in 1993 by Jeff Sutherland, John Scumniotales, and Jeff McKenna at the Easel Corporation. It was inspired by the ideas presented in a 1986 Harvard Business Review article, *The New New Product Development Game*, which emphasized flexibility and iterative progress. Scrum was formally introduced to the world when Sutherland and Ken Schwaber presented their paper, *The SCRUM Development Process*, at the OOPSLA (Object-Oriented Programming, Systems, Languages & Applications) conference in 1995. This system focused on short, iterative planning cycles and adaptability, laying the groundwork for many modern project management practices.

Agile came later. In 2001, a group of software Engineers, including Scrum pioneers Ken Schwaber and Jeff Sutherland, created the Agile Manifesto, outlining principles for better software development practices. What I like most about Agile is that it steps all the way back to our mindset and approach before it jumps into practical steps. Take this manifesto, for example:

Manifesto for Agile Software Development

We are uncovering better ways of developing software by doing it and helping others do it. Through this work, we have come to value:

- Individuals and interactions over processes and tools.

- Working software over comprehensive documentation.

- Customer collaboration over contract negotiation.

> • Responding to change over following a plan.
>
> That is, while there is value in the items on the right, we value the items on the left more.[8]

This manifesto was a public declaration of a policy that all software developers should implement. It was a gathering of founders in the software development field that wanted to find the right way to work together as a team on ambiguous projects. I loved that it didn't say what to do, just what they valued more. This was a powerful way for my mind to think about processes and systems in a new way. Task management and scheduling didn't have to be as rigid as Waterfall with its step-by-step functionality and lists of dos and dont's. Instead, the production pipeline could be founded on a set of values that everyone respects and aims for.

When I work with game development teams, I make sure to remind them of the Agile manifesto, as it lays the foundation for our values. The best part is discussing this with the team, and if they agree or disagree, we can change it however we see fit. The goal is for them to see how flexible our task management system is, rather than viewing it as a rigid process that enforces exactly what I say.

Let's take it a step further. My mind is always on comparisons to video games. So I just had to make our own take on this for the video game producers of the world to enjoy.

---

8   Beck, Kent, Mike Beedle, Arie van Bennekum, Alistair Cockburn, Ward Cunningham, Martin Fowler, James Grenning, et al. *Manifesto for Agile Software Development.* Agile Alliance, 2001. https://agilemanifesto. org/.

> Manifesto for Agile Video Game Producers
>
> We are uncovering better ways to enjoy games by playing them and sharing our experiences. Through this, we have come to value:
>
> - Jumping quickly into gameplay over story setup.
>
> - Intuitive controls over reading lengthy manuals.
>
> - Quick load times over in-game advertisements.
>
> - Second-to-second gameplay over pay-to-win experiences.
>
> While the items on the right serve their purpose, we prioritize the items on the left.

If we want to make public declarations about the policies and values we want to see in our craft, why not make our own? When we need a north star to point toward, we can ask ourselves a set of questions like this and prioritize our values.

Getting back to Scrum, it was not created as a separate system from Agile. Instead, Agile adopted Scrum as a practical framework that fit within its philosophy. Scrum uses iterative planning and short development cycles called sprints. These cycles help teams maintain a steady workflow by breaking large projects into structured phases. Each sprint sets clear goals, allowing teams to review progress frequently and adjust their plans when necessary.

Before diving into the mechanics of Scrum, it is important to introduce the role of the Scrum Master. The Scrum Master serves as a "servant leader" for the development team. Their job is to coach the team within the Scrum process and help with communication and eliminating roadblocks. Instead of acting as a traditional manager, they focus on empowering the team and creating an environment in which work flows efficiently. Sound familiar?

My first certification process for Scrum introduced me to the term "servant leader," which led to my deep dive into Greenleaf's teachings. For the full circle, Scrum Master is another role and function a video game producer can take on while on a Scrum team. Some of the key aspects to being a Scrum Master include:

- **Focus on team needs** - Their main goal is to empower the team to self-organize and work toward their goals, not to dictate actions or micromanage.

- **Removing impediments** - They actively identify and address any roadblocks or challenges that will hinder the team's progress.

- **Coaching and mentoring** - The Scrum Master provides coaching and support to team members, helping them develop their skills and guide them through the Agile principles.

- **Facilitating Scrum events** - They ensure that Scrum ceremonies like daily stand-ups, sprint planning, and retrospectives are conducted effectively and productively.

- **Promoting transparency** - They strive to create a culture of openness by making information about the team's progress, like status reports.

- **No direct authority** - Unlike a traditional project manager, a Scrum Master does not have hierarchical power over the team, relying instead on influence and collaboration to achieve results.

With that understanding in place, we can now transition into the five key steps of the Scrum process. This is where the Scrum Master plays a vital role in facilitating each stage. Note, however, that these steps are for creating a task management system around a project that already has clearly defined goals.

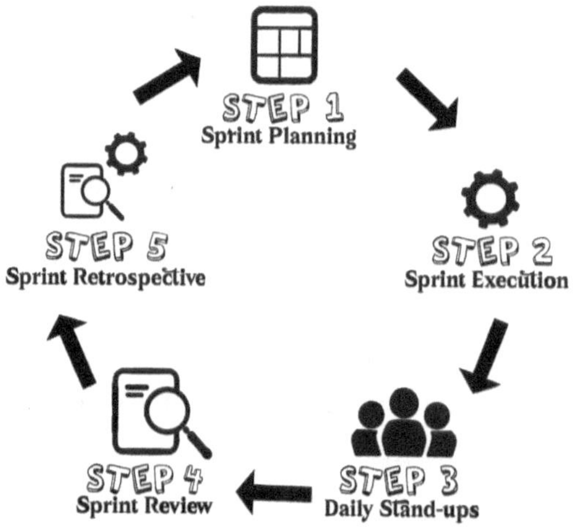

1. **Step One: Sprint Planning**

   This is where the team decides what they will accomplish during the sprint, with the sprint being defined as a set period of time (usually one to four weeks). The team collaborates to select the most important or feasible tasks from the backlog and clearly defines what "done" means for each task.

   The Scrum Master helps guide this conversation, ensuring that the goals are realistic and aligned with the project's priorities.

2. **Step Two: Sprint Execution**

   Once the sprint begins, the team focuses solely on completing the planned tasks. The goal is to deliver a functional increment of the project by the end of the sprint. Everyone knows their role, and the team works together to meet the sprint's goals.

The Scrum Master ensures that distractions are minimized and that team members have what they need to execute effectively.

3. **Step Three: Daily Stand-Ups**
   These are short, daily meetings (often 15 minutes) in which team members share progress, discuss roadblocks, and align efforts.

   The Scrum Master facilitates these meetings, keeping them focused and productive.

4. **Step Four: Sprint Review**
   At the end of the sprint, the team demos the completed work to stakeholders and receives feedback. This is the moment to evaluate whether the sprint's goals were achieved and to show off what has been built.

   The Scrum Master ensures that the review process is constructive and that feedback is captured for future improvements.

5. **Step Five: Sprint Retrospective**
   After the sprint review, the team reflects on what went well, what didn't, and how to improve it for the next sprint. This step is about learning and evolving the process for future iterations.

   The Scrum Master plays a key role here, encouraging open discussion and helping the team identify ways to work more efficiently in the future. They create a safe space where others can speak their minds freely about improvements.

Understanding the Scrum Master's role in this process is crucial. Their focus is on enabling the team, not controlling it. Like a skilled raid or squad leader, the Scrum Master keeps communication flowing and removes obstacles that slow down progress. They ensure the team stays focused and productive, helping them work toward shared goals.

In a game production setting, the team might decide during Sprint Planning (Step One) to focus on adding a combat feature in which the fighter performs a backward kick that knocks enemies back. The sprint is dedicated to building only that feature, ensuring the team is not overloaded with additional tasks. Sprint Execution (Step Two) begins as the engineers and artists start creating and testing the feature. During Daily Stand-Ups (Step Three), the team discusses any issues, such as animation glitches or code conflicts, and adjusts their approach to stay on track.

By the time the sprint ends, the backward kick feature has been developed, tested, and reviewed. During the Sprint Review (Step Four), the team presents it to stakeholders and gathers feedback for possible refinements. Finally, the Sprint Retrospective (Step Five) gives the team an opportunity to assess how the process went. They evaluate the effectiveness of their planning, identify obstacles that caused delays, and refine their approach for the next sprint. All of this force multiplication for the team is being done by you, following those simple five steps of Scrum.

This iterative process ensures steady progress while allowing teams to make necessary adjustments. Unlike Waterfall, in which late-stage changes can be expensive and disruptive, Scrum allows for continuous improvements throughout development. Teams can focus on immediate goals while maintaining a clear vision of the project's overall direction.

People gravitate to Scrum because it is built around sprints. Each sprint locks in a set amount of work, creating checkpoints before the next phase begins.

A common saying in Agile and Scrum is to picture yourself taking one step forward, stopping, and asking, "Am I going in the right direction?" If the answer is yes, take another step and ask again. If not, determine the correct path and adjust before moving forward. Each step represents a sprint, ensuring progress is measured and intentional. In this way, a video game producer can outline tasks and hold their team responsible for deliverables.

This brings up another important element of task management: determining how long tasks are going to take. To understand how much work fits into a sprint, or how long it will take to complete an entire project in Waterfall, producers rely on estimation. Regardless of whether you are working within a structured plan like Waterfall or an adaptive framework like Scrum, estimating work timeframes is essential. It allows video game producers to track progress, set priorities, and keep overall development on schedule. From managing a single sprint to overseeing an entire production cycle, understanding the scope of work ensures a balanced workload and proper resource allocation.

Let's explore what it takes to estimate effectively and why it is one of the most important skills in video game production.

ESTIMATING

The early morning air was cool as the farmer walked the rows of crops. Some were just sprouting, and others were nearly ready for harvest. The day before, Mayor Lewis had arrived with a request. The town needed 100 units of a single crop, all shipped by the end of the season. With 30 days to complete the order, the farmer knew this was a test of planning.

Wisdom dictated that the first step was to check how long crops take to grow. Spring offered several options. Cauliflower needed 12 days. Green beans kept producing, but required extra time before the first harvest. Garlic and other crops varied in speed. Potatoes, however, stood out. They harvested in just six days. That made them the easiest and safest choice.

The farmer mapped out the plan and considered their options.

A single planting of 100 potatoes would be too risky, because it would take so long to water them all at once. If anything went wrong, there wouldn't be time to fix it. Instead, planting in four smaller batches of 25 meant a steady supply. With each batch taking six days, the entire order would be completed in 24 days, leaving six days as a buffer. The plan was simple and reliable. Seeds went into the soil, water followed, and every few days, another set of crops reached harvest. By the end, the crates were filled, and the order was completed ahead of schedule.

Stardew Valley is a relaxing game where players manage a farm and build relationships with the villagers. Estimation happens automatically in your head as you farm and watch your crops grow. Every action takes time, and planning ahead helps each season run more efficiently.

When we play video games, estimation is everywhere. We constantly ask ourselves, "How long will that take?" Games show us progress bars and countdown timers, helping us track growth, crafting, or experience points. In RPGs, every match or battle tends to grant experience points, letting players estimate how much more is needed to level up. It happens instinctively, whether you are farming crops or preparing for the next adventure.

An essential attribute for everyone, including video game producers, is the ability to anticipate when tasks will be completed, which we do through estimation. **Estimating** *is the process of predicting the time, cost, or effort needed to complete a task or project based on available data and past experiences.*

Think of any game that you play. If I asked you any of these questions, you would be using estimation to determine the answer:

- How long does it take to beat the final level?

- How many monsters do you need to kill to level up?

- What is the fastest way to travel?

- How long do you play each day?

As video game producers, estimation is one of the top skills we need to perform with our development teams. This skill is similar to foresight, which we've previously looked at, but it additionally allows us to plan for the future in a more scientific way. Just as a player would in a game, a producer can break down a list of tasks and estimate how long each will take in order to understand how much time is necessary to achieve the final goal.

The following thought process is a helpful starting point for making estimations:

- Plan.

- Make Decisions.

- Set Expectations.

- Avoid Problems.

Before estimating how much time something is going to take, you need to make sure you understand the project itself. You walk through the project's necessary steps in your head and make a plan to accomplish it. By making the best decisions along the way, you set expectations for the possible outcomes and avoid problems to the best of your ability. Planning helps teams break down work into manageable steps. With a solid plan in place, a producer can estimate how much time and effort different tasks require, and use that information to create schedules for their team. However, with good estimates, each of these four thought processes becomes easier to iterate on and accomplish.

The farmer used data from the test crop to decide when to plant, how often to harvest, and whether to stagger plantings for added flexibility. The ability to make good decisions becomes easier with good estimates. Teams can weigh what's possible against what's too risky. If something looks like it will take too long or cost too much, they can adjust before committing resources to that part of the plan. The farmer had multiple crop options but chose potatoes because of their short growth cycle, which allows multiple harvests. This reduced the risk of relying on a single planting.

Expectations improve when teams know how long things will take. The farmer knew exactly when each batch would be ready, so there would be no uncertainty when Mayor Lewis checked on the order. The shipment was delivered early, with confidence instead of guesswork.

Avoiding problems is one of the biggest benefits of estimation. Things rarely go exactly as planned. Estimating allows teams to build in extra time and flexibility, preventing last-minute failures. The farmer didn't plant everything at once. Instead, crops were staggered, ensuring that, if something went wrong, there was still time for another round. That buffer removed the risk of missing the deadline.

Understanding estimation makes work more predictable, reduces risk, and allows for adjustments before problems arise. Whether on a farm, leading a raid, or managing a development project, good estimation ensures that goals are met without unnecessary stress.

Estimation Benefit	Raid Leader	Squad Leader	Video Game Producer
Planning	Estimates how long a raid boss fight will take and organizes team rotations for healing and damage output.	Plans how long it will take to capture an objective and prepares for reinforcements.	Estimates development timelines to ensure teams stay on track for milestones.
Decision Making	Decides if the team should push forward or reset based on how long it will take to recover from a wipe.	Determines whether to hold position or advance based on enemy reinforcements and supply availability.	Weighs the risks of adding new features based on time constraints and available resources.
Expectation Setting	Communicates how long each raid phase will take so the team knows when to use cool-downs.	Provides a timeline for an assault so that teammates can coordinate movements.	Sets clear timelines for stakeholders on when content will be completed and delivered.
Avoid Problems	Builds in extra preparation time, in case of raid wipes or unexpected mechanics.	Plans for delays by setting fallback positions and backup strategies.	Accounts for potential delays by including buffer time in the production schedule.

Once you have thought through these four points, it is essential to share them with everyone involved so that the shared vision and understanding remain the same. But, more importantly, how do you estimate things that you do not yet know how to estimate? If I said, "Make me a brand new game feature that will drastically impact the game you are working on, and tell me how long it will take," how do you answer that?

By nature, we often measure time in days, hours, minutes, and seconds. For example, baking a cake might take an hour, and a commute to work could take 30 minutes. These are units of time, also known as time intervals. We use these when we have a general understanding of how long a task takes.

However, creating a video game for the first time is a lot like playing a game for the first time; there are many unknowns. No one truly knows how long something will take, because it is a brand-new thing we are creating for the first time. This uncertainty makes estimation a challenge. Video game producers use techniques that game developers (and even players) can adopt when trying to estimate unknowns. They use generalized terms or references. The two common approaches you will see in game development teams are:

- **T-shirt sizing**: To give a broad sense of scale, tasks should be categorized as small (S), medium (M), large (L), or extra large (XL).

You force yourself to categorize them into one of these sizes. I've been on teams where small (S) is similar to a day task, and Extra-Large (XL) means multiple months. The beauty is that your team gets to determine what it means.

- The **Fibonacci Sequence**: Using values like 1, 2, 3, 5, 8, 13, and 21 to estimate effort, recognizing that larger tasks have greater uncertainty.

The Fibonacci Sequence is effective for estimation because it encourages relative sizing of tasks rather than precise time estimations. This system reflects the inherent uncertainty in complex projects by using progressively larger gaps between numbers as tasks become more difficult, which prevents teams from getting caught up in overly detailed calculations and promotes a more realistic understanding of the effort required.

The key to implementing these frames of reference is repetition. By consistently applying these methods with your team, you develop a shared model of understanding the scope and effort, and can thus improve estimation accuracy over time.

In game production and project management, estimating plays another equally vital role.

One of the most important tools for managing estimations is the **Iron Triangle**, *a concept that balances scope, time, and cost to predict and influence quality*. You are thus able to provide three different types of estimations that help you understand your quality potential.

- **Scope** *refers to the amount of work being done. Are you building a small feature, or is this a massive, AAA game project?*

- **Time** *is the amount of time you have to accomplish the work. Are deadlines tight, or do you have the flexibility to deliver at a steady pace?*

- **Cost** *is the required resources, money, personnel, or materials.*

The idea is: you can't change one without impacting the other sides. If you want to increase the scope, the sides of the triangle will also need to be adjusted, and you'll need more time or money. If you want it done faster, you might need to reduce the scope or increase the budget. It's a great reminder that everything in a project can impact each other, thus varying our estimations.

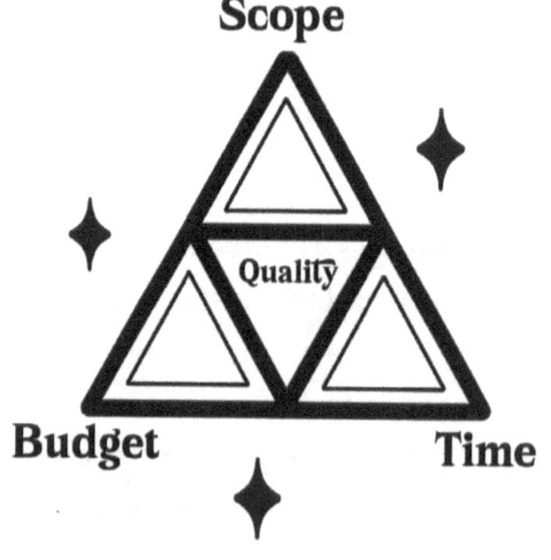

Focusing on cost is important, but often overlooked by our profession. Video game producers typically do not manage budgets directly, but their estimates provide Studio Leadership with the data needed to make financial decisions.

Layoffs in the industry have become more frequent, making accurate cost estimation even more critical. Recognizing financial risks early can help prevent projects from exceeding budgets and keep teams stable. By effectively estimating these factors, producers and teams maintain realistic goals while balancing quality. This skill mirrors the decision-making players use in games. Both require strategic thinking and careful trade-offs to achieve the best possible outcome within set constraints.

In the upcoming section, we will look at another hidden talent that video game players have developed. I find this one the most impressive skill of all, and it can directly influence the improvement of our estimations and how fast we can get our work done. Ever heard of Speedrunners?

SPEEDRUNNING

The year was 1997, and *GoldenEye 007* had just launched for the Nintendo 64 in August. The allure of James Bond had been a staple of my childhood. Every weekend, my grandmother would take us to Blockbuster, where my brothers and I would carefully choose a classic James Bond film to rent. With his sharp wit and suave demeanor, Sean Connery was our favorite. We were captivated by larger-than-life villains like Jaws and Oddjob. Along with the movie, we'd grab a box of buttery popcorn, and then hurry home to dive into the world of gadgets and iconic one-liners.

When *GoldenEye 007* came out, it was like a dream come true: a chance to step into Bond's shoes and live out the action. The game quickly became a centerpiece of our weekends. Its second mission, "Facility," stood out as both thrilling and frustrating.

The mission takes place in a chemical weapons plant, just like at the start of the film. The game gives you a set of tasks to follow, such as locating a scientist and retrieving a keycard from him. Then, you set explosive charges while facing an army of guards and navigating a labyrinthine layout.

What made *GoldenEye 007* especially intriguing was its system of unlockable cheats, tied to completing missions within certain time limits. If you could beat "Facility" in under two minutes and five seconds on the 00 Agent difficulty, you'd unlock the coveted "Invincibility" cheat. It seemed downright impossible for a group of kids like us. We could never beat it in under three minutes.

The problem was our approach. Like most players new to the game, we thought the key to success lay in meticulously clearing every room of enemies. Guards were stationed at nearly every turn, their machine guns trained on you the moment you stepped into view. We tried everything. Memorizing guard placements, practicing our aim, and running through the mission over and over. Yet, we could never get our run under three minutes.

One weekend, while flipping through a video game strategy guide, we stumbled upon an article that changed everything. It explained the secret to completing the level in record time.

The key wasn't in fighting the guards or meticulously completing objectives. It was in ignoring them entirely. The magazine revealed that, to beat the time, you had to sprint past most of the guards, avoiding unnecessary combat, and prioritize retrieving the scientist's keycard. The keycard itself could spawn in one of two locations, adding an element of chance to the run. Once you had it, you simply ran to the exit without looking back.

It was a revelation. The idea of avoiding combat and focusing purely on efficiency felt counterintuitive. Growing up, every action movie or game had taught us that success came from defeating the enemies in front of you, from clearing the way to your goal. But this? This was different.

The notion that the most effective way to complete a mission could involve running past machine-gun-wielding guards without firing a shot was both bewildering and fascinating. When we tried it, the mission was transformed. We no longer saw the level as a series of encounters to overcome but as a puzzle to solve. We analyzed the layout, noting every path and shortcut.

> Which doors opened the fastest?
>
> Where could we cut corners?
>
> Could we avoid triggering certain guards altogether?
>
> Each run became a calculation, every second shaved off an exhilarating triumph.

Who would have foreseen that a whole community and sport would start to popularize behind this genre of gameplay, and call itself Speedrunning. **Speedrunning** is *a timed playthrough of a video game or a portion of a video game, completed as quickly as the player can.*

Speedrunning did not just start with *GoldenEye 007;* it was considered as soon as the first games were made. *Dragster* by Activision on the Atari 2600 back in 1980 might be the very first popular speedrunning game that players would discuss. Players attempted to get the fastest time in a drag race, with recorded times printed in magazines for others to emulate and beat. With the accessibility of the internet In the 90s, game legends like *Doom* (1993) and *Quake* (1996) started to garner online communities who would share files and speedrun results. Now, this type of gameplay has been popularized all over Twitch and YouTube for some of the most intense, clever, and efficient ways players have come up with to beat their favorite games.

When you understand the concept of speedrunning, you realize that to some degree, everyone unintentionally plays games that way. This means that every gamer, including you, is already practicing this skill of focused efficiency every time they game. In *GoldenEye*, to get a fast time, I didn't engage every guard or complete every objective in the way you'd expect. Instead, my speedrunning success was due to finding the most direct route to the exit and executing it with precision.

That day, when we finally beat the mission in under two minutes and five seconds, the feeling of elation was unforgettable. The invincibility cheat was ours, but the real victory was the knowledge we had gained. *GoldenEye* had taught us to see beyond the obvious, to question the constraints we placed on ourselves, and to approach problems creatively and precisely.

These types of speedrunning perspectives led me to Jeffrey Liker's *The Toyota Way*. This book delves into Toyota's Lean Principles, a system that revolutionized both management and manufacturing.

Manufacturing companies have developed powerful frameworks, such as the Lean Principles, to eliminate inefficiencies and refine execution to the smallest detail. The way speedrunners analyze routes, remove unnecessary actions, and find the most efficient path mirrors the way businesses streamline operations to maximize output.

Lean *is about eliminating waste, that is, anything that slows you down without adding value.* Imagine playing a game with unskippable cutscenes, long load times, or useless side quests that don't help your progress. Lean thinking removes those inefficiencies, keeping only what helps you reach the goal faster. It streamlines processes so that every action contributes to progress. In gaming terms, it's like refining a speedrun by removing unnecessary movement and optimizing every input.

Then there's Six Sigma, a similar system developed by Motorola. **Six Sigma** *is about reducing variation and ensuring consistency.* Six Sigma applies statistical analysis in order to identify errors and improve quality.

Over time, the two systems have been gently merged together to form **Lean Six Sigma**, *a methodology that combines Lean Manufacturing's focus on waste reduction with Six Sigma's emphasis on eliminating defects and improving quality.*

Let's compare Lean Six Sigma's two complementary philosophies:

Methodology	Focus & Goal	Speedrunning Gaming Analogy
Lean	Eliminating waste Maximum efficiency.	Skipping cut-scenes, avoiding unnecessary battles, and using shorter text strings to progress dialogue faster.
Six Sigma	Reducing variability Consistent results.	Making your travel path between villages take the optimal route.

At the heart of it, Lean Six Sigma is a system designed to cut out inefficiencies and create repeatable success. Instead of making random changes, it follows a step-by-step process that ensures improvements last. Lean Six Sigma provides a universal way to solve problems and refine workflows. It does not rely on rough guesses or trial-and-error. Every step is intentional, ensuring that changes are backed by real data and tested solutions.

Within Lean Six Sigma, specifically Six Sigma, there is an easy acronym to remember the steps of its process: DMAIC. The **DMAIC (Define, Measure, Analyze, Improve, Control)**

methodology *follows a structured approach to improving performance.*

This mirrors the mindset of speedrunners. Let's explain:

1. **Define** - Identify the goal.

2. **Measure** - Track performance.

3. **Analyze** - Find the bottlenecks.

4. **Improve** - Optimize execution.

5. **Control** - Maintain consistency.

As a speedrunner, the first step is to define what we are trying to achieve. Some runs focus on completing only a level or an entire game within a set time. Others add extra challenges, such as finishing with specific restrictions or avoiding certain mechanics (e.g., avoiding extra fights by evading guards in GoldenEye *007*).

To keep things simple, let's focus on beating the entire game from start to finish as fast as possible. With this goal in mind, let's go through the DMAIC methodology.

- Define: How fast can we beat the game?

Once we have a goal, we need to measure how our current outputs are performing. A baseline helps us understand our starting point and how consistent our runs are. Without knowing our current baselines, it will be impossible to track if we are progressing later on.

- Measure: I can beat the game in 10 minutes flat.

With a baseline in place, the next step is to analyze that time. Where are the biggest slowdowns? Are there specific levels or sections that take longer than expected? Do we make mistakes at certain points that could be avoided? Identifying these areas helps us focus on where improvements will have the most impact.

- Analysis:
    - Level 1: 2 mins (0 retries)
    - Level 2: 5 mins (2 retries)
    - Level 3: 3 mins (0 retries)

Now that we know where the biggest challenges are, we can start improving. If the second level is the hardest and takes the most time, that is where we need to focus our improvements. Improvement is all about testing different approaches and seeing what works best. We know what works best when it consistently improves over our baseline.

- Improve:
    - Level 2 New Time: 3 mins (0 retries)

Finally, once we see progress, we need to control and sustain those improvements. A single fast run does not mean much if it cannot be repeated. Consistency matters. Practicing the new strategies ensures that the time stays low and that mistakes are reduced.

- Control: Reach consistent outputs of 8 minutes to complete the entire game.
    - Level 1: 2 mins (0 retries)
    - Level 2: 3 mins (0 retries)
    - Level 3: 3 mins (0 retries)

From there, the cycle continues. We establish a new baseline, analyze what needs to improve next, and keep refining. There is always room for improvement, and we can keep on reducing the time it takes to beat each level. Each pass through the process makes the run smoother and more optimized, bringing us closer to a perfectly executed speedrun.

DMAIC: Steps to Perfection Compared

Phase	Lean Six Sigma Example	Speedrunning Example
Define	Define what success looks like for a project.	Complete a level in under a specific time.
Measure	Gather metrics to establish a baseline.	Use splits and timers to measure progress.
Analyze	Analyze processes to identify bottlenecks.	Review video footage to find where time was lost.
Improve	Test and refine solutions to eliminate inefficiencies.	Find a faster route or refine inputs.
Control	Put systems in place to maintain improvements.	Develop the ability to beat a level consistently with the same process.

Let's apply this methodology as a video game producer. Since Lean Six Sigma was developed in the manufacturing industry, it is not yet widely used in the gaming industry. But we have an opportunity to show that Lean's value is not dependent on the industry, and I think implementing it with my team's quality assurance testers and engineers proves that.

I worked at a studio where they were going to develop a game similar to *World of Tanks*, but set in outer space, called *Dreadnought*. The players in that game were running into serious problems connecting to servers and finding matches with other players. Some couldn't connect to matches at all. Others were waiting far too long to find a game. Even when they did get in, the teams felt unbalanced. It was clear the system had issues that needed urgent attention.

I worked with the studio's QA team first to help define the problem. They outlined the biggest pain points based on player reports and from their own internal testing. Players were struggling to connect, which was causing high queue times, creating a bottleneck, and causing other backend infrastructure services to fail.

- **Define**: Fix matchmaking queue times to prevent bottlenecks and downstream impacts.

Next, we needed to measure how bad the situation really was. The QA team dug through past test logs, and it became clear that matchmaking hadn't been getting enough focus. Out of 1,500 test cases per build, only 300 targeted matchmaking. Among those tests, we noticed that many players who had failed to find a match or faced long queue times also had large inventories to load into the game. This meant they were loading in with unexpectedly large file sizes. Imagine having to carry a backpack with all your belongings everywhere you go. You would get tired just like our backend system.

- **Measure**: How long does it take to load into a game with a small inventory as opposed to a large inventory?

Once we had the data between the two different types of inventory sizes, we could see how much of an impact they were causing. Once we had that data, we were able to test our theory with a proper analysis.

- **Analysis**: If players had more than 100 items in their inventory, their log-in times backed up the queue.

Now that we had data from the measurement and our analysis of that data, we could focus on improvement. First, we worked with the engineers to see if they could optimize the servers that maintained inventory data for the players. If we could make the transfer of that data more efficient, we could potentially prevent the bottleneck.

- **Improvement**: Reworked the server backend read and write database to query the information faster and not cause a bottleneck.

Finally, we needed to make sure that we could control and sustain these improvements. We built digital dashboards on our internal tools to monitor connection success rates and matchmaking stability. Successful connections jumped from 70% to 95%, and match start times dropped below 90 seconds. By tracking efficiency scores, we found even more ways to refine our testing process, ensuring that these improvements stuck.

We also introduced a dedicated matchmaking testing suite focusing on the biggest issues first. Automated tests replaced slow manual ones, cutting down the time it took to verify connections. Stress tests were added to simulate real-world conditions, ensuring we caught problems before launch. We also created a priority bug queue so that matchmaking issues could be fixed faster.

With the problems improved, the team also saw the value in using Lean Six Sigma methodologies. Process improvement can be applied to almost anything. This got me thinking about how we actually do apply process improvement in our daily lives, at work, and in our video games. Process improvement is just a mindset, and Lean Six Sigma's DMAIC steps are an easy, effective way to make improvement a reality. Once you have mastered that mindset, I think it opens up Pandora's box with respect to the way we should approach things.

For me, learning this system felt like I had unlocked a secret ability inside my brain that I had been mastering in video games for years. This led me to view my skills in a whole new way, and I think it applies to all gamers. What if thinking about things in an analytical way and being hyper-focused on details in the subconscious of your brain could enable you to achieve greater success? What if it let you win video games or naturally beat them with faster times? Let's dive deeper into this secret ability you've been mastering inside the games you already play.

GAME INTUITIVE MINDS

Speedrunners are analytical and detail-oriented so that they can pull off the level of performance needed to hit their goals. They have a special talent for problem-solving, which is why they excel at both breaking games down and pushing them to their limits. Even if you are not aiming for a speedrun, you likely utilize these same skills every time you game. What if we identified what was really happening here and finally give it a name? Don't worry, I already did. **The Game Intuitive Mentality** *is the ability to recognize when something behaves unexpectedly and figure out how to use it advantageously.*

This separates casual players from those who truly understand how games function. Some players stumble upon exploits by accident, while others test mechanics intentionally to uncover new possibilities. This level of awareness requires deep attention to detail, and I believe it can be applied to our job as video game producers, not to mention everyone on a game development team.

Have you ever played the original *Pokémon Red and Blue*? If you did, you might have heard about MissingNo., one of the most famous exploits in Pokémon history. Players found a way to encounter this glitch Pokémon by manipulating the game's data in a specific way.

By following a series of steps, they could force the game to generate MissingNo., a graphically broken Pokémon on the coast of Cinnabar Island. Interacting with it would cause other strange graphical errors, but the real draw was the item duplication glitch. By performing this trick, players could create unlimited Rare Candies, Master Balls, or any item they wanted.

It's fascinating how intuitive players were to find the exact steps required to pull this off. Here's how they did it:

1. Go to Viridian City and talk to the Old Man who teaches you how to catch Pokémon.

2. After you finish his tutorial, fly to Cinnabar Island without entering any battles.

3. Once on Cinnabar Island, use the Surf ability and move up and down along the right edge of the island, staying within the water boundary.

4. Eventually, you will encounter MissingNo., or another glitch Pokémon, depending on your name's specific data values.

5. If you have a specific item in your sixth inventory slot, encountering MissingNo. will multiply it up to 128 times, giving you an infinite supply.

Were these players just lucky to stumble across this? In a sense, yes. But they also paid attention to what was happening and figured out how to manipulate and replicate it. This is exactly what having a Game Intuitive Mentality looks like. Instead of playing a game exactly as intended, they asked questions.

What happens if I do this?

Can I manipulate the game to get a different result?

They weren't just playing *Pokémon*; they were exploring its inner workings with an intuitive mind.

Let's address the elephant in the room when it comes to words like *manipulation* and *exploitation*. These terms can often carry a negative connotation, as we discussed in the three types of power, but in the context of games, they describe a way of thinking that focuses on problem-solving and discovering how systems work. There is a moral responsibility that comes with using these techniques, and the results should always lead to something positive.

If an exploit or technique is used in a way that takes advantage of others or negatively impacts the game for players, it crosses the line.

Some glitches are harmless, while others can ruin experiences for those who are playing as intended. If what you are doing is causing frustration, unfair advantages, or harming a game's community, the intention is no longer about learning. At that point, it becomes unethical, and it is time to stop. A Game Intuitive Mindset is about curiosity, not abuse. It is about testing the limits of what is possible while respecting the game and its players. Always keep that in mind when applying these techniques.

Another compelling example of intuitive thinking in games

is found in *Minecraft*, where players have constructed functioning computers and circuit boards within the game world itself. *Minecraft's* block-based, pixelated graphics allow for deep mechanical complexity, enabling players to focus on creating intricate systems. Central to this is a material called redstone, which works similarly to electrical wiring in the real world. Players can place redstone on the ground to connect components, creating circuits that transmit signals and control various actions. By using additional components such as repeaters, comparators, and special torches called redstone torches, players can direct and modify these signals. Together, these components form simple logical systems known as logic gates. Logic gates allow players to control how signals behave, making basic decisions or computations. Examples include gates named AND, OR, and NOT, which determine if a signal should pass through based on certain conditions. This forms the fundamental building blocks for creating more advanced circuits, such as computers and automated systems within *Minecraft*. Yes, a computer inside a video game.

Through these components, players have developed fully operational 8-bit computers capable of executing basic programs. These in-game computers can perform tasks like arithmetic calculations, data storage, and even display outputs on redstone-powered screens. This showcases an intuitive approach to gameplay, where players not only engage with the game mechanics but also explore and manipulate them to create automated systems. It exemplifies the Game Intuitive Mentality, that is, understanding a game's underlying systems and leveraging them in innovative ways to achieve new functionalities.

You are probably starting to see how this kind of curiosity can be applied to far more than just video games. Let's take a look at how this mindset can level up a video game producer. I applied it with my game development teams while working with artists on *Rocket League's* arena and map designs. This wasn't about taking advantage of a system in the game. It was about refining a workflow process to make development smoother and more efficient. *Rocket League* has seasonal content; releasing a new map or arena with every season was the goal. Creating a map takes significant work. The process requires a team to build 3D assets, set up lighting, and apply effects.

Originally, this workload was managed by three to four people. However, when our team was downsized, we were left with only one artist to create maps each season. But our leadership team still wanted us to continue to output the same number of maps each season. We had to rethink how to approach map production without sacrificing quality. We started by analyzing what took the most time to build in each new area. Together, our team approached the problem with an open mindset and determined that we should kitbash. Kitbashing is the process of combining parts from other maps to create something new. This would drastically reduce the time required to create brand-new 3D models. We could reposition, resize, and retexture objects to give them a fresh look, while ensuring the environment still felt unique. It might not have been the highest-quality approach for the players of our game, but it was a way for us to ship something rather than nothing.

Another great example of the Game Intuitive Mind also comes from *Rocket League,* and it was a free win for the game design team. *Rocket League* has a mechanic called a Flip Reset that allows a player to extend their air time by using the jump ability twice. This was not supposed to be possible, as the player's car was supposed to touch the ground with all four wheels before the jump ability resets. However, players discovered you can reset your jump if you are mid-air and can lightly touch all four wheels of your car on the ball you are dribbling. This movement takes skill, but it resets your jump without touching the ground and gives you an instant advantage. This was actually a bug, and the designers did not intend for this functionality to happen. Rather than fix this "bug," the Game Director decided to use the community discovery to their advantage and keep this functionality. It was a fun and inventive use of the game; it required skill to pull off, and the community loved it. This was an amazing decision in hindsight because of the extra level of player expression this one bug helped create for the community.

If a team is going to reach its full potential and develop a Game Intuitive Mindset, the producers and other leaders must recognize what each person needs to succeed. To approach things with a curious, intuitive mindset, individual team members must be in a place to do their best work. Enabling a team to work from this mindset is one of the most powerful experiences a producer can create, and it's worth knowing how to build and protect this space.

In the next section, we will take a look at another pyramid, known as *Maslow's Hierarchy of Needs*. This tool helps a producer know when to step in and support a team member before personal or life challenges become a roadblock. People need a strong foundation before they can aim for higher goals. If someone seems disengaged, it may be because they don't feel secure in their role. If a team is struggling to collaborate, there may be a lack of shared direction. A producer who picks up on these signals can step in before minor issues grow into major setbacks. And a producer who can create a space for Game Intuitive Minds to flourish is creating a space for powerful and effective momentum toward the shared goal.

MASLOW'S PRODUCER

The *Sims* is a beautifully crafted series that has been at the forefront of creative freedom and expression in real-life simulation games for decades. The ability to be someone different or to try out different lifestyles in a digital world is what draws everyone in. Taking care of your Sim becomes a point of pride, and you build a relationship with your digital avatar.

In the game, you can do most activities that you can do in the real world. You can socialize and go to parties, work and progress in your career, and customize and build your home with amenities like pools or different technology, such as TVs and computers.

When I started playing *The Sims,* I think I made the same mistake as many others. I used it as a creative outlet to be someone different, and I wanted my Sim to have a party lifestyle. My Sim was going to be the coolest, get all the nice clothes, and go dancing at everyone else's house or club. When you start the actual game, you don't have enough money to buy cool clothes or do whatever you want. The first thing you need is a job. That makes sense, so you sign up for one. After your Sim gets home from work, you think, *"Finally, we can do something fun together."*

Before you can even start, a stomach-growling sound plays, and a warning pops up. Your Sim is hungry. Fine, I can wait to shop. Eating comes first.

You take care of that, then finally get online to browse the Sim Mall. Just as you start looking for new clothes to purchase, the Sim makes a strange noise. A bathroom warning appears. Fine, go to the bathroom. Now, can we get back to shopping? As soon as you sit down, the Sim lets out a deep yawn. A sleep warning flashes on the screen.

The reason The Sims is so enjoyable is its creative freedom. However, when simulating real life, you still have to follow the rules of being a human. Abraham Maslow, a famous psychologist, hopefully everyone remembers from grade school, found a clever way to visualize this.

He devised a pyramid in which the base of our survival and basic needs must be solid before we can ascend to the peak of self-actualization.

Self-actualization, *the realization and fulfillment of one's talents and potential, especially when seen as a fundamental drive or need within everyone.*

When you consider what video games offer, it's an intriguing lens through which to explore this idea. In games, you don't usually need to worry about the bottom half of this pyramid, so does that mean you reach Self-Actualization faster in games?

At their core, games are designed to empower players. When you enter a virtual world, the constraints of reality are left behind. There are no bills to pay, and no bad weather to stop you from doing something outside, just the freedom to act, experiment, and explore. It's this sense of freedom that makes video games so engaging. **Empowerment** *is about instilling a sense of value in someone, giving them the autonomy to make their own decisions and chart their own course.*

Why does empowerment feel so natural in most games? It's because they remove the real-world barriers we face every day. In life, you can't focus on personal growth until your fundamental needs like food, shelter, and security are met. In most games, you don't worry about how to keep your character fed or housed unless the game deliberately makes it part of the experience, as in *The Sims*.

For me, this idea of self-actualization isn't just about individual success. I don't even like to frame it that way. My mindset is always on the team setting and how to serve the vision. It's about the ability to see through misdirection and recognize the team's shared vision. I want to get to the top of the pyramid, not as a solitary achievement in growth, but as something we accomplish together because we all want to. "There is no I in Team," as the saying goes.

I was playing a ton of *World of Warcraft* raiding with a guild that had a steady but diverse group of gamers for over a year. We had several different, distinct personalities, age groups, and differences in financial success. We were just a mix of people coming together for the love of a game and to overcome its challenges together. During this time, I was also working as a producer at a development studio, where we won contracts and signed deals with other game studios to support their projects. Since I had been working at that development studio for so long, I could also see the distinct different personalities, age groups, and differences in financial success among my coworkers. Noticing the similarities between the two groups, I started to wonder whether I could apply the way I treated my guild to how I treated my team at work. In *World of Warcraft,* I supported my successful team by ensuring their well-being and needs were taken care of so we could win our raids. Why wouldn't working in a game development studio be any different in supporting one another so that we all succeed?

The stronger the team becomes, the more we all gain. "A chain is only as strong as each individual link," as the cliché goes. That's where servant leadership comes in again. Robert K. Greenleaf's words resonate deeply with me:

> *"The servant-leader is servant first... It begins with the natural feeling that one wants to serve, to serve first. Then conscious choice brings one to aspire to lead."*[9]

I hope we all find the feeling of wanting to serve each other to level up the entire group. I am not the first to explore these questions, and I was grateful to find the works of psychologists and motivational thinkers like Robert Greenleaf and Abraham

---

9   Greenleaf, R. K. (2016). *The Power of Servant Leadership.* Brilliance Publishing.

Maslow. As a result, I kept reading and also discovered thinkers like William Ouchi and Frederick Herzberg. Each of them developed theories about what motivates teams, which I found fascinating and interlinked. When you combine them all, it can't be just a coincidence; this is the key to what leadership should focus on when taking care of their teams.

I believe we witness their theories while playing with other players and, in some cases, even in heavily story-driven single-player experiences. In the next section, I'll break down how these frameworks intersect and why they matter for producers looking to build strong teams.

Maslow, Herzberg, Ouchi, and Greenleaf have shaped how I understand psychology and leadership. They each studied different aspects of motivation, but they all identified the same universal truth about how teams succeed. People need a strong foundation, as depicted by the base of Maslow's pyramid, before they can perform at their best. Without that, you will just become our favorite *Sim* character in the story before getting burnt out. To start with, let's look at the base structure of Maslow's Hierarchy of Needs again.

- Food, Water, Shelter

- Security and Stability

- Love and Belonging

These are great needs, but as a video game producer, how are you responsible for making sure that people have food, water, and shelter? How do you provide security and stability? And when it comes to love and belonging, isn't that something only the HR Department should handle? Relationships in the workplace and video games are not the same as in personal life, right?

Yes, and no. An effective video game producer is not fully responsible for their coworkers in this way. But we can offer support to get our team higher up the pyramid and able to produce their best work by ensuring that those needs are met and truly understood. Let's see how Maslow's Team addresses this.

There is a pattern I want to show you that will hopefully become self-evident. Every one of these psychology leaders is talking about the same thing, but from a different angle or approach. To create a satisfied workforce, basic needs must be met first. Both Frederick Herzberg and William Ouchi recognized this in their research. Their theories explain why job satisfaction requires more than just a paycheck and why companies must consider both stability and motivation.

Frederick Herzberg developed the Two-Factor Theory, which separates workplace factors into two categories. The first category, called *hygiene factors*, includes salary, work conditions, and company policies: the good stuff that everyone loves when it exists. These create a stable environment in which employees feel secure. However, they do not lead to long-term motivation.

The second category, known as *motivators*, includes recognition, achievement, and personal growth. These create job satisfaction and drive employees to perform at their best. Without the hygiene factors supporting your teams, dissatisfaction will grow among them. But without motivators, work feels unfulfilling.

This is a pretty cool concept, but let's make it even more relevant. How can we understand the Two Factor Theory in video game terms? If we think of hygiene factors for games that we play, what is our core baseline expectation? We would assume the game we play doesn't crash and has stable performance. We want the UI and HUD elements to be easy to read with controls and inputs that are responsive. These are some fundamental aspects we, as players, expect to be present in a playable game. The absence of these elements creates frustration. That being said, their presence doesn't necessarily make the game enjoyable either. Just like a job's salary or work conditions don't make a job fulfilling.

Motivators are going to be the long-term enjoyment in our games. These could be meaningful progression systems to level up our characters or get stronger weapons. This could also be achievements and recognition on leaderboards or trophy systems with gameplay that has creative expression. These motivators are the things in games that keep you playing, and without them, you likely wouldn't stay.

Let's take a look at a similar idea from William Ouchi, who introduced Theory Z, a blend of Japanese and American management styles.

William Ouchi developed Theory Z in the early 1980s after studying Japanese companies (Toyota, Nissan, Matsushita, etc.) and comparing them with U.S. companies. In the decades after World War II, Japan rebuilt its economy with a strong focus on stability and community, while the United States pursued rapid growth and individual achievement. These differences in national culture shaped how businesses operated and how employees related to their companies.

In Japan, companies emphasized lifetime employment and a strong community. Workers often spent their entire careers at one company. In return, the company took care of them with stable jobs, housing support, social clubs, and a sense of belonging.

Ouchi's idea with Theory Z was simple but powerful. If companies want long-term loyalty, they cannot just demand it. They have to earn it through consensus at the top, with shared decisions that make employees feel included and respected. Once employees buy into those decisions, they give their individual determination and hard work because they feel the company has invested in them and values their input.

In games like *EVE Online* or *Runescape*, players make a huge time commitment to build their characters and carve out a place in the world. Guilds and player communities often take on the role of supporting that investment. They maintain shared resources, such as crafting stations or guild banks, so that basic needs are met and everyone can focus on progressing together. Many groups also practice patience with inactive members, keeping them in the guild even if they have been away for weeks, because they trust that the player will return. This mirrors Theory Z, where long-term loyalty is earned through shared responsibility and care for the community, which in turn inspires players to keep contributing their time and effort.

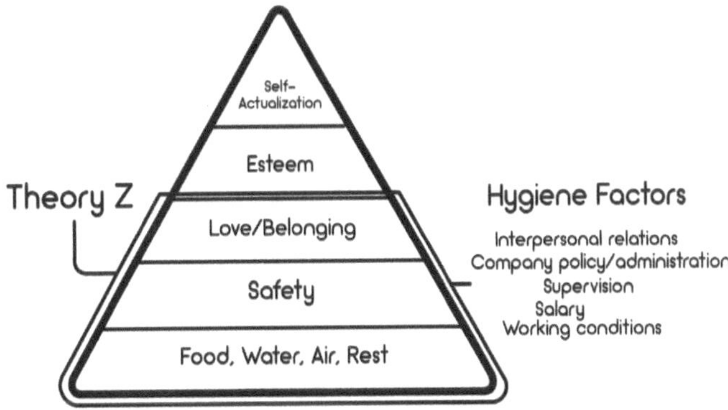

Both theories are connected to Maslow's hierarchy of needs,

as they are all focused on the bottom half of the pyramid. The consistency around this topic is astonishing. It's important to understand how these work if you ever want to find motivation for yourself or for your teams.

How a Team Addresses the Base of the Pyramid:

- A team that ignores these foundations risks losing employees to stress and dissatisfaction.

- A team that provides them creates an environment where workers can reach their full potential.

- A team that wants innovation must first ensure employees feel secure. If someone is struggling with job stability or basic needs, they will not be able to focus on high-level problem-solving or creative work.

Maslow describes this as being unable to reach self-actualization. Herzberg sees it as motivation being blocked by workplace frustrations. Ouchi frames it as employees being unable to commit fully to the company's goals.

No matter how it is described, the message is clear. If you don't address a team's fundamental needs, higher-level success will be out of reach. Modern technology and many game companies recognize this issue and have taken steps to reduce stressors that interfere with productivity.

Many offer office spaces with food lockers, on-site cafeterias, and amenities that make daily life easier. Some prioritize competitive pay and work to establish offices in locations where housing is more affordable. These efforts help employees focus on their work without worrying about some of the bottom half of Maslow's Pyramid's basic necessities. While perks can improve the work environment, they do not replace core needs like financial security, career stability, and fair treatment.

Companies that balance stability with motivation create workplaces in which employees can succeed. They provide a safe working environment so teams can focus on innovation. They also go beyond this to make workers feel valued and engaged, not just supported.

Now, let's add another layer of complexity. What about those who do not share your background or perspective? Just because you have a specific need or something works well for you doesn't mean that others have the same experience. Leadership is not just about applying what works for you. It is about recognizing what your team needs and finding ways to support them. (Think back to that Hammer and the Screws analogy).

During my time in the military, I saw a half-solution implemented to address this challenge. The military is known for treating all service members as equals, regardless of sex, religion, creed, or politics. The focus is on the unit as a whole, ensuring that soldiers work together and support one another. This is great in theory, but in my opinion, they enact it in the most extreme way possible.

The military provides everything you need in Maslow's Pyramid, but it forces you out of Self-Actualization and coercively molds you into their own actualization. They need you to be a soldier, so they make you one, which I agree with. Troops must remain cohesive and follow orders without hesitation. That structure requires setting aside personal goals and focusing entirely on the mission.

In the classical sense of an army, individual choices are limited because maintaining discipline is a priority. This is why the military does not truly emphasize the highest level of Maslow's pyramid, *self-actualization*. Soldiers are trained to put the needs of the mission first, and you can't have that mindset with a self-actualization approach. To be fair, soldiers are not just robots; they are trained to make their own decisions and to show initiative, but this is not entirely what I am talking about.

Good news! Game studios are not set up like the military, and neither is the civilian world. People are motivated by more than just survival and duty. If we want to build teams that thrive, we need to recognize what individuals require to perform at their best. To build that strong foundation, we need to ask the right questions:

Are team members being compensated fairly and given the resources they need to focus on their work? The living conditions and financial stability of team members do matter. Leaders don't need to know personal details, but they should be aware of whether employees feel secure in their daily lives.

Do people feel safe in their environment? Stress and uncertainty can impact performance. Of course, we should always have literal safety, but feeling unsafe due to more nuanced factors can happen far more frequently than we might realize. No one should feel discriminated against, pressured, overlooked, or taken unfair advantage of.

Is there a sense of belonging within the workplace? Strong teams build camaraderie through trust and respect for everyone. This can get eroded if team members start to form cliques, sometimes referred to as "The Old Guard," a group of people who are the inner crowd, while newcomers are not yet welcomed in.

If any of the team's answers to the above questions are negative, you need to try to solve it or escalate it to higher leadership that can solve it. This is servant leadership at its finest, identifying what your team needs and taking action. Speaking of servant leadership, I want to bring Greenleaf's teachings back into the discussion. His work provides a way to turn these ideas into action. By focusing on the needs of others, leaders create workplaces that encourage both personal and professional growth.

Greenleaf explains how leaders can actively support their teams by addressing their core needs. The ten principles he identified with Larry Spears guide leaders in creating an environment in which people feel valued. A leader who takes the time to listen and build connections thus fosters a culture where teams feel supported and stay motivated. Once these servant leadership concepts are fully understood, we can begin applying them to improving team performance at any level of the pyramid.

This is the beauty of Maslow's Team: seeing all these concepts and theories fit together like perfect puzzle pieces. On their own, each of these concepts has been written about and philosophized in great detail. But, outside of Maslow's Hierarchy of Needs, I have never seen them put together in a way that demonstrates how these important puzzle pieces work together toward the shared vision of the whole. For a video game producer, your job is to make sure your team's needs are taken care of so that each individual can produce their best work.

But, unfortunately, just understanding the principles and trying to implement them might not always work. When that happens, I use two specific techniques to help gain alignment and resolve conflict with others. These techniques were things that I have been doing my entire life, and I never knew what to call them. The first is actually a Japanese gardening technique. The great minds behind this technique noticed that gardening strategies can help business culture align teams in a harmonious way, ensuring decisions have buy-in before they are fully implemented. The second focuses on the power of relationships and the influence of certain connections in creating lasting benefits. This one is a Chinese business philosophy that has been in practice for hundreds of years.

Let's look at these in more depth, starting with gardening.

NEMAWASHI

As a Healing Officer in my guild, I often found myself navigating conflicts to maintain harmony between all the team members. My role was to organize and oversee the healers for our weekly raids, ensuring that we executed healing rotations tailored to each boss's mechanics. Some encounters required rapid-response AoE (Area of Effect) heals to sustain the entire raid, while others demanded powerful single-target healing to keep the tank alive and protected from direct damage. The success of our raids depended on the healers working as a team so that the rest of the raid members could trust that we would heal them back up when they took damage. If players panicked and ran, it only made things worse, straining the tanks and making healing unpredictable.

However, two of our top healers, Becca and Mink, were

constantly at odds. Becca favored assigning dedicated healers to specific roles, keeping two healers focused on the tank and two healers on the rest of the raid.

By contrast, Mink believed having two healers on the tank was a waste, arguing that one was sufficient. He wanted the other three to keep the rest of the party alive, with one main healer calling out when others needed support. Their disagreements disrupted our preparation time and sometimes carried over into the raids, creating an awkward tension that affected the entire team. They were both exceptional healers, but their inability to align was becoming an issue that competed with the shared goals of the guild: to have fun and win raids.

The breaking point came while we were preparing for a difficult raid boss. This boss fight had multiple stages, and one of the biggest challenges was dealing with waves of "adds." These are smaller enemies that appear before and during the main boss fight, acting as guards or minions and diverting our attention until we can defeat them. Once the smaller enemies were gone, the team could shift its attention to the boss, but that required a different attack strategy.

As usual, during our planning session, Becca wanted to assign two healers to the tank while the other two focused on keeping the rest of the group alive. Mink advocated for his alternative system, and the discussion quickly turned into an argument. Both were convinced their approach was correct, and neither wanted to change their stance.

Instead of forcing a decision in front of the group, I decided to let it play out one more time. After that raid, I had a strategy I wanted to implement, and I was pretty sure it would work to get them aligned. In the days leading up to our next raid, I spoke with Becca and Mink separately. My goal was to hear their reasoning, understand their concerns, and help them see a way forward that would work for everyone.

First, I met with Becca. Before our conversation, I had a strong feeling that she and Mink were closer in their thinking than they realized. Their disagreement seemed bigger than it actually was. If they had the chance to talk through their ideas, I had a feeling they would probably find common ground. My goal was to get them to have that conversation, and then gently guide it in a way that helped them see where their strategies overlapped rather than focusing on their differences.

Becca shared her frustrations and explained why she valued structure and predictability. She felt that a detailed plan reduced mistakes and made sure everyone was accountable. I acknowledged her points and emphasized how her method brought stability to the team.

Then I shared examples of past encounters in which being flexible had helped us succeed. I saw her start to reconsider her approach. By the end of our conversation, Becca agreed to allow some flexibility in her plans as long as the team stayed organized.

Next, I sat down with Mink. He believed that strict plans failed to account for unexpected changes. He preferred to trust his instincts and react quickly when situations shifted. I told him I understood his perspective and reminded him how his quick thinking had helped the team in the past. Then, I explained that having a simple plan in place would cut down on confusion, giving him more freedom to focus on making the right calls when it mattered. I also told him that his callout system for healers was a great way to keep resources balanced. He started to see structure as a tool that could support his instincts. By the end of our conversation, Mink agreed to follow a basic plan that kept the team organized. If a situation called for more flexibility, the team would have a clear way to decide when to shift from the plan and adapt as needed.

When I brought them together, there was no need to negotiate. The plan was already in place; this was now just an acknowledgement for everyone else. I went over what they had agreed to in our earlier conversations to ensure everything was clear. Becca's structure would keep things organized, and Mink's callout system would allow flexibility when needed. They both nodded, seeing their ideas reflected in the plan without feeling they had to give anything up. The meeting was quick and simple, confirming what we had already worked out.

On raid night, the results were instantaneous, and everyone in the raid recognized it. With Becca and Mink in sync, we set the example of working together, and even our healing improved. Everyone was aligned as if it were everyone's idea.

What I learned from this experience was the importance of preparing people for change. By listening to Becca and Mink individually and gradually introducing their perspectives to one another, I had created an environment in which collaboration could take root. This groundwork laid the foundation for trust and alignment between them.

What I was unknowingly doing with my raid team was similar to the concept of *nemawashi* (根回し is pronounced "neh-mah-wah-shee").

In Japan, *nemawashi* is a term borrowed from gardening that refers to carefully preparing a plant for transplant by gradually introducing its roots to the new soil. This ensures the plant has time to adapt to its new environment without shock or damage.

In a broader context, **nemawashi** describes *laying the groundwork for change by engaging with individuals informally and gathering support before publicly presenting an idea or decision.*

> ## Nemawashi
>
> Is slow to consensus but fast at executing.

In Japanese corporate culture, *nemawashi* is an important part of decision-making. Before an idea is formally proposed in a meeting, it is discussed informally with certain key people (stakeholders). These smaller conversations allow concerns to be raised, feedback to be gathered, and alignment to happen first. By the time the meeting happens, most of the major decisions have already been made, making it easier to move forward without conflict.

This is a simple but powerful technique. Besides using it in MMOs as a Raid Healing Officer, I have also used this technique working as a video game producer. For instance, I applied this approach when I worked on the publishing side of a game studio. There are two teams needed to launch and support a game successfully: Development Teams and Publishing Teams. Sometimes they work under the same roof, and sometimes they are separate companies. When these teams do not interact frequently, they can become misaligned with the shared vision for the game.

Development includes the designers, artists, and engineers who build the game itself. They focus on creating worlds, characters, and gameplay. Publishing includes marketing, community management, and partnerships. Their job is to make sure the game reaches players and builds an audience. Each team needs the other to succeed because, at the end of the day, money keeps the studio running and paychecks coming in.

As a publishing producer, I worked closely with the publishing team to identify opportunities to grow our game's presence. One of the biggest ideas we had was to expand our partnerships with major sports organizations, such as the NFL and MLB. These leagues were super supportive, and our player base responded well to them. It seemed like an obvious win.

The development team had other thoughts. They weren't excited about bringing outside brands into the game. To a development team, especially artists, it doesn't feel creative to copy and paste someone else's work. They pursued game development to design their own worlds, not to recreate existing ones. They worried that working on partnership content would take time away from more exciting projects and limit their ability to be innovative.

To be fair to the publishing team, they didn't want to force these partnerships onto the developers either. The goal was never to take away their creativity but to show them why these collaborations mattered. We were running a business and needed to make a profit to sustain an active, loyal player base, whether the economy was good or bad. If we could find a way to make both teams happy, the whole studio would benefit in the long run.

I intuitively knew that if we just threw both teams into a meeting, it would turn into a debate rather than a solution. So I used *nemawashi* and started meeting with each side separately first, without letting the other side know.

I first met with the development team to understand their concerns. They explained that working on partnership assets felt tedious. When using another company's brand, every small detail had to be exact and specific to the brand specifications rather than to the game itself. Any mistake led to revisions, and the process often felt like it was more about following rules than creating something meaningful. They didn't enjoy spending time on tasks that required approval at every step, instead of focusing on their own designs.

However, they were open to the idea if the work could be handled in a way that didn't slow them down and if they could still do their own original IP work.

Then, I met with the publishing team. I explained that the developers wanted the game to succeed, but also needed room for creative work. They were willing to work on partnership content if they had more flexibility in the designs. If the partners agreed upfront to loosen brand restrictions, the process would move faster and feel less like busywork.

The publishing team understood this and saw the value in adjusting the approval process with outside brand partners. They were open to working with these partners to set clearer expectations, ensuring the collaborations fit within the development team's creative freedom. By the next partnership deal, the process had improved.

When we eventually brought both teams together to discuss this partnership, the publishing team told the development team that the license holders had agreed to give the creative team more flexibility and limit the number of required approvals. The development team was on board, seeing this as the right way to handle these deals moving forward. Both sides now felt the process was set up for success.

This conversation, which could have been very inefficient, turned out to be focused and productive. The development team supported the partnerships, as asset creation would now move faster without unnecessary delays. The publishing team committed to sharing performance data so developers could see the impact of their work.

In the end, the balance worked. The assets fit into the game without limiting the development team's creative work, and the partnerships performed well, earning profits for the studio. The response from players was the ultimate factor in establishing that it was a positive event for everyone, as they cheered about it online.

By preparing for these conversations ahead of time, the transition to alignment was harmonious. What could have been a difficult debate became an easy agreement, all because both teams had the chance to align before the meeting.

In video game production, *nemawashi* isn't about avoiding disagreements. It is about creating a process where alignment happens harmoniously and collaboration feels seamless.

By engaging teams individually and preparing them for compromise before the big decision meeting, producers can turn potential conflicts into opportunities for agreement and alignment. This technique makes sure that every voice is heard first before introducing it to conflict. Thoughtful groundwork isn't just a tool for transporting plants from one area to another or for getting two top MMO healers on the same page; it is the foundation of strong leadership and trust.

Building alignment is one thing, but maintaining lasting relationships is another. *Nemawashi* helps set the stage for smooth decision-making that leads to alignment, but it makes it a lot easier if you have strong relationships with those other team members right off the bat. Working on your relationships and understanding the power of them is something that isn't often discussed. There is a simple term in Chinese called *Guanxi*, which translates to relationships. It also has an interesting background and lessons from Chinese business culture we can discuss further in the next section.

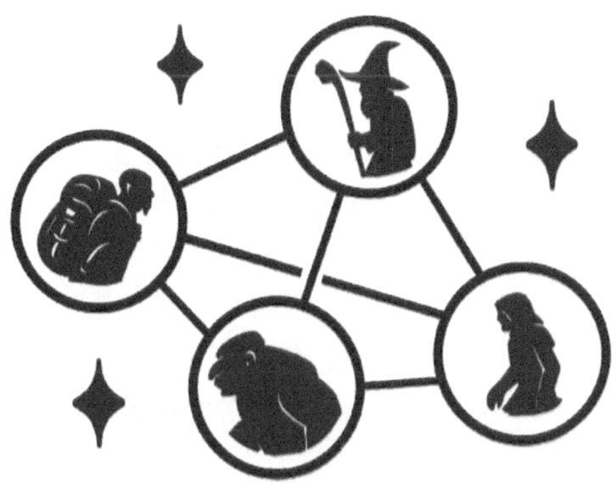

GUANXI

The sound of clanking armor and murmured conversations came through the speakers. I was slumped on the couch, observing my friend's favorite character just walk into a medieval town, with every NPC turning to watch him pass by. A blacksmith waved him down. A shopkeeper called him by name. A guard gave him a respectful nod.

"Okay, that's weird. Why is everyone treating you like the mayor, and where did all these new NPC animations come from?"

"Because I basically am," he said, not looking away from the screen. His character moved with easy confidence, like a man who owned the place. "Check this out! I get discounts and free stuff, and even the guards are my friends. They remember all the good stuff I've done for them." I looked over to see that he had an actual look of appreciation on his face.

Slightly teasing, I said, "Hey buddy, you are getting way too excited about your fake friends here. They're programmed to act like that after you finish a quest." I saw a slight shake of his head. Which caused me to quickly follow up, "It's still impressive, but...it's literally part of the game."

He didn't respond, keeping a determined face as he led his character into a shop. The moment he stepped inside, the shopkeeper started to animate, cheering and clapping for my friend. He immediately pointed at the screen, "Look! Look! Look!"

The NPC Shopkeeper started a new voiceline, "Ah! My best customer! Here for another deal? Anything in the shop, you get a special price."

I stared at the screen. "Wait, what? He's giving you a custom greeting here, too?"

"Yup."

"That's not normal. I never get that."

"Because you..." He paused for a moment and then, with a nonchalant voice, said, "You never did anything for him. I saved his kid from a den of necromancers. Now he hooks me up anytime I stop by." I squint at the screen. "Okay, yeah, that's... pretty cool. But that's just a quest reward. It's not like he actually knows you; you don't need to call him by name."

He grinned. "Alright, you wanna see something crazy? Watch this!" His character turned, then stepped outside to run through the city gates and past the gate guards. "Watch how much the guards love me. See that monster up ahead? I can just stand here and be perfectly safe. Guard Jones always protects me."

I pressed a hand to my forehead. "Why do you know the NPC guards by name?"

He responded quickly, sounding offended, "Yeah, man. That would be disrespectful to Guard Jones if I didn't. He seriously protects me all the time." Before I could argue, the monster lunged forward. My friend's character didn't move. A heartbeat later, Guard Jones rushed in, sword drawn, and took the hit like it was his sworn duty. Another guard joined in. Then another. They cut down the beast in seconds. My friend's character remained untouched.

I let out a slow sigh. "Guard Jones is kinda badass."

He yelled, "HELL YEAH HE IS."

We both laughed.

Video games do a great job of showing that helping other people matters and building relationships with them is just as valuable as everything else we do. The quest system is built around this idea. You complete a task, and, in return, you gain something useful, like gold, experience, or access to the next part of the story. Some NPCs have no gold to give, but you increase your relationships with them through reputation. The higher the reputation you earn, the more discounts they might offer at their shop or share hidden knowledge that helps later on in the game.

At first, this looked like a simple game mechanic, but as I kept watching my friend, I realized it was something more. Helping others and forming connections changed how the game world responded to him. It was just like building up a network of people in the real world. How often do you turn to your friends and family for recommendations, advice, or borrowing a random tool?

It was trying to understand the significance of strong relationships, which led me to the Chinese concept of guanxi, *a network of personal relationships and the obligations and influence associated with them.*

Pronounced *gwan-chee* (关系), this concept is a core part of Chinese business culture. It refers to networks built on trust and mutual support. While it is often translated as "connections" or "relationships," these words do not fully capture its depth. *Guanxi* is more than just knowing people. It is about forming authentic, long-lasting bonds that create opportunities and stability for both parties. The roots of *guanxi* go back to a time before formal banking systems, when communities relied on direct trust to manage trade and cooperation.

Imagine a fishing boat captain arriving in a new village, unfamiliar with the area and without any local contacts to introduce himself to first. The village will want his fish, and he will want to sell it. To build a relationship with a local contact, he might offer a nice, friendly discount or other acts of service in the hope of demonstrating his willingness to form a long-term relationship with them. The fisherman gains a trusted partner, and the villager secures a mutual relationship with a new source of food. This is *guanxi* in action, where both sides benefit from cooperation and relationship-building to strengthen their bonds.

Though *guanxi* is built on trust, it also has complexities.

The reliance on personal relationships can sometimes blur the lines between ethical cooperation and favoritism. The fishing boat captain is not expected to offer acts of service or discounts, as the city does not allow any fishermen to set up in the markets. Some may use *guanxi* in an exploitative way, to gain unfair advantages, such as securing special treatment based on personal ties and gifts rather than merit. This is wrong. If you see this, it needs to be called out and stopped.

In video games, some of the best examples of *guanxi* are working with other players who are focused on crafting. In some games, it might be difficult to gather materials and craft. An example would be gathering flowers and herbs that you will need to create potions at an alchemy station. If you need materials to craft the potions, it might be good to know someone who gathers the materials and build a relationship by showing you are kind and willing to share potions. This isn't supposed to be quid pro quo; it's about finding people in a network who want to work together.

Here is an example of how people can abuse the power of a relationship with other players in-game that you might have come across as well. Imagine a scenario in our MMO raiding guild. A 20-person raid is scheduled, but 25 guild members want to participate that night. If *guanxi* is misused, some members might try to gain favor with the guild leader by giving excessive gifts, such as potions, rare crafting materials, or in-game gold.

Instead of earning their place by following the guild's rules and waiting their turn, this creates a system in which personal favors matter more than skill or contribution. This kind of favoritism weakens trust and damages the group. Leaders who allow it to happen manipulate the system by adjusting rules to benefit certain players over others.

Persuasion cannot justify these actions because they are not based on fairness or honest decision-making.

True *guanxi* is built on trust and consistency, not on using relationships for personal gain. When favoritism takes over, it becomes a system where power is traded rather than relationships built on mutual respect. The strength of *guanxi* comes from its authenticity. It works when relationships are based on trust and mutual support, not manipulation. Some people choose not to engage in these kinds of relationships, and that is also fine. No one should feel pressured to return a favor, and there should be no resentment if they don't. It simply means that this is not the type of connection they want to build.

As a video game producer, I look for this trait in others, not just in myself. I will bend over backward to support another team member in any way I can, as long as I know they would do the same for me. Everyone has heard of the golden rule, "Treat others as you want to be treated." That is the true part of being on a team, wanting to have a relationship of giving with each other.

Working on a development team, your goal is to build your *guanxi* with your entire team so that you can help each other out when you need to. I usually earn my *guanxi* and relationships with my teams by protecting them as new feature requests come in by implementing production taskmaster systems so that they don't get hit by everything at once. In return, I have relationships with engineers and artists that can help me gain access to certain parts of the game for triage when I need assistance or a quick question. We have a relationship where we can reach out and ask each other questions, and neither of us is bothered by these requests.

As we reach the end of Part One, I hope it is becoming clear that video game producers do more than manage tasks and act as a coordinator for the team. They set the tone for the team and help create an environment where trust grows. That sometimes means going the extra step without expecting anything in return.

Being a Servant Leader is not about working for others. It is about working toward something greater. If I see a teammate struggling because important documents are disorganized, I don't leave them to figure it out alone. I step in and organize the information, regardless of whether my guanxi will increase. This is not because I expect a favor later on, but because it helps the team move forward. Every time I do this, I reinforce something simple. Helping people out of kindness strengthens relationships.

This idea extends beyond personal interactions. If I am a producer working with engineering teams, I should want to build a strong relationship with QA. That trust becomes a foundation for better teamwork. Conversations flow more easily. If I need insight, I can ask without hesitation. When people see you as part of the same team, they want to help. This is not because they have to. It is not because they owe you anything. They do it because they trust and respect you. And that is the real strength of *guanxi*.

With a strong understanding of leadership and managing, we are now ready for Part Two, where we will focus on working within different types of teams as a producer. This will be a fun look at what life is like in a game studio, but we will still rely on your inherent knowledge as a gamer. Some companies or studios are comparable to large guilds in an MMORPG, while others are small and mobile, like the team in a small shooter. And some companies feel like Bowser's kingdom because they fall apart when their leader disappears. Others are more like Princess Peach's kingdom because they stand the test of time. Even *Pokémon* applies here, as we will look at how diverse teams have advantages. Let's jump into it!

PART TWO - THE TEAM

One of the most exciting things about joining a guild was the opportunity to raid. In *EverQuest*, raiding wasn't just about challenging content and boss mechanics. It was a massive undertaking that required dozens of players working together and listening to the other raid leaders. Raids weren't small-scale encounters in *EverQuest*. At the time, they were some of the largest battles that brought together over 50 players, sometimes even 100+, all pushing toward a single in-game boss.

In 2002, the *Planes of Power* expansion for the game introduced one of the most complex raid progressions in MMOs. Players had to battle through a series of high-level zones, each themed around powerful gods, before earning the right to enter the ultimate endgame challenge, the *Plane of Time*. This final zone was where the highest-level players faced off against some of the hardest bosses in the game. For many players, merely reaching it was a badge of honor.

This expansion came out around the time when I was introduced to the game. I was playing with my school friends and my brother in a guild we joined after meeting some people online. The guild was called Eternity's Reign. It was an exciting time in my youth, not only for joining the guild and raiding, but because I got to spend so many hours at home getting to play with my brothers, and we now had our own personal computers to play on. My brother and I recreated our local *Counter-Strike* cybercafe experiences by playing next together, but now we had computers on opposite walls in our home living room.

EverQuest felt like stepping into an entirely new world, with the different races and classes we were playing with. Up until this point, we had been playing in small groups to level up and gain experience, usually playing with five or six people to clear out small dungeons. Now, instead of participating and managing just one group, we were in a guild. We would be working with several groups to make up a massive raid party. It was no longer just about how well we played as individuals in small group combat. This was my first experience outside of school to see an organization operate from the inside and to follow precise strategies alongside players who had been mastering these systems for months or even years before me.

The guild raided every Friday night, and it was obvious that new members were expected to participate consistently. Showing up seemed simple enough, but actually being prepared was another story. I'd never really had to prepare for a raid before, and even in school, I was always the back of the class type of guy, trying to keep my head down, so I had no real-world experiences to relate to it either. I had no idea what I was walking into.

Our Guild Leader, Volaki, was also our Raid Leader. The moment everyone logged in, he started directing us through the chat box in-game. I happened to be away from my desk and in my kitchen. In the guild chat, he typed out, "Alright, you all know where we're heading; it's been posted on our bulletin board, which I linked out earlier today. Let's run out and meet up there." Suddenly, everyone started riding off, including my brother.

I wasn't completely negligent here; I had clicked on the url earlier and read the board, so I knew we were heading to a Dragon in the Wakening Land. I just had no idea where that was. My plan was just to follow everyone lurking in the back. At this time, voice communication tools were very limited, and we weren't using any. Also, EverQuest did not have a map system; you couldn't look at an in-game map and figure out where to travel to. You used an in-game compass. Or you had to Alt-Tab to minimize the game and look up guides on websites like allakhazam.com.

The good news was that I had my brother playing with me just in the other room. I yelled, "Hey, where did you guys run off to?" He yelled back, "I have no idea! I just started following, and we're running through a forest. It's just trees everywhere!" I didn't want to be *that guy* who immediately asked obvious questions. Frantically, I tried to follow the group, but the problem was that they scattered around a corner before I could catch up. I typed a message to my friends, "Where are we going? What's happening?"

No response.

Dread crept in as I hesitated before finally typing into the guild chat.

"Hey, sorry, everyone, where are we going?"

Almost immediately, one of the senior guild members messaged me. To my surprise, it wasn't annoying or dismissive. It was friendly.

"Hey, no worries. I'm coming back so you can follow me."

Impressed, I made a mental note. *He is a helpful person.*

We arrived at the destination, a cave where the guild planned to pull the boss out to a safer area for the fight. Raiding itself was surprisingly simple in concept. Everyone gathered in the center of the forest on a slight hill. The typical process was that a player with a crowd control class, usually a Monk, ventured out to lure in the boss. Bringing the boss back to a controlled location made the fight more manageable.

This allowed us to avoid dealing with the boss's guards or any additional NPC minions who might complicate things. While this process sounds straightforward, the anticipation made every second feel monumental. It was also interesting at the time, as it was my first time seeing so many players working together toward a single goal.

A message popped up from a new, different person to me, one of the Senior Clerics in the guild.

"Hey man, it's nice for you to join us. You are going to be grouped with us and the rest of the Clerics. Do you know what a complete chain heal rotation is?" For the second time that night, I froze. I hesitated before responding, embarrassed and completely unprepared.

"Not really," I replied. I had my eyebrows raised and was side-eyeing the chat, knowing he couldn't see my facial expressions.

"No worries," he said. "I'll keep it simple. When the boss comes in, *FeralXWarr* is the one taking all the hits. Our job is to make sure they don't die. That dragon hits hard, way harder than a single heal can keep up with. So instead of spamming heals whenever, we take turns. One Cleric starts casting, then a few seconds later, the next one starts, then the next. That way, every time the tank gets hit, there's already a heal on the way."

I knew that *Complete Heal* takes ten seconds to cast. That's a long time in a fight where the tank is getting hit constantly. If only one Cleric tried to heal, the delay would be too long. A second too late, and the tank could drop before the heal landed.

To stop that from happening, we would stagger our casts. The first Cleric would start, then five seconds later, the next one would begin, then the next. That rotation guarantees a *Complete Heal* every five seconds, which perfectly heals the tank's health, so that it is bouncing between full and nearly dead each time.

The time between heals will actually change between bosses to match damage outputs. It was just five seconds for this particular boss.

The more I listened, the more I realized how much coordination it took. The strategy sounded simple, but every healer needed to stay focused and keep track of timing, so they knew when to cast the next heal. If someone panicked or cast too early, the whole rotation could fall apart.

The Cleric continued, "We don't just time it by instinct or counting in our heads. We set up auto-message macros to make sure everyone stays in sync. When I start my cast, my macro sends a message in party chat. It'll say something like, 'Starting *Complete Heal*, next up in five seconds is Cleric #2.' That way, the next Cleric knows exactly when to go."

The rotation kept repeating that way. Each time a Cleric cast, their macro would trigger another message. When cleric #2 started his cast, his macro would call out, "Healing in ten seconds, Cleric #3, you're up in five." Then, when Cleric #3 started, his macro did the same for the next person. That way, everyone knew exactly when to start without having to guess.

Some Clerics kept their messages straightforward.

Others threw in jokes or dramatic one-liners, but the structure stayed the same.

No matter how it was phrased, the system worked because everyone followed the timing. As long as each cast happened at the right moment, the tank wouldn't drop, and we never had to scramble to fix a bad situation.

At the time, I didn't even know what systems were. This was an ingenuity I hadn't realized could exist in a video game. I wasn't just witnessing a strategy. I was seeing human systems with Game Intuitive Mindsets in action. This was my first time experiencing how teams functioned on such a large scale and came up with their own strategies that the game designers did not intend players to do. It appeared that everyone had a role, and the entire group moved as one, with purpose. Each doing their own strategy and contributing in their own ways.

After the raid, my brother and I sat down to talk about everything that had happened. Healing had so many moving parts. The rotation, the timing, the macros, and making sure every cast lined up. It felt like learning a whole system just to do the job right.

Since the Warriors were in the middle of the fight, I asked what his role was like.

He just laughed. "Nothing. I literally stand there and auto-attack the boss in the back." That was all there was to it. No complex timing, no coordination with other Warriors, no strategy like the Clerics had. Healing required constant awareness and communication. His role was about standing in place and swinging.

That first raid was fun and unforgettable. There was so much more to learn, and the thought of improving felt exciting. Contributing more meant earning better loot, but more than that, it meant being part of something bigger. The raid members were prepared to help newcomers onboard; they knew how to get me up to speed on their systems, and I saw how people listened to coordination with respect to the raid leader.

This was a fast transition from working in a small party to being part of a guild and experiencing large-scale coordination for the first time. It was my first real exposure to participating in a video game group of this size, and I was only just beginning to understand how these communities functioned and the parallels to the real world and industry.

Part Two of this book is about focusing on the team. The lessons now shift from personal leadership and production fundamentals to understanding the different types of teams and companies you will encounter as a video game producer. The experiences shared here reflect what it is like to work in a studio, from how teams are structured to the dynamics that shape their success.

Looking back at my first raid, I wish I had known how similar these organizations were to the teams we work with in the gaming industry. The structures, the leadership styles, and the challenges all reflect what happens in game development.

This section will explore the different team types you can expect, from small indie studios to large AAA companies. We will look at how team culture and policies shape the ways that people work together and how those choices can either strengthen or weaken collaboration. We will break down the roles of stakeholders and team members, so you know what to expect when working with them.

Finally, we will put it all together and discuss how teams function on large-scale projects, such as creating a video game. We will look at what it takes to align a team toward a common goal and why morale and motivation are just as important as deadlines and production schedules.

Let's begin by looking at the different types of teams you might encounter.

TEAMS

Video game players have a unique perspective on teams because of the countless interactions and scenarios we have participated in compared to the average person who just plays on a sports team. Whether in online multiplayer or single-player campaigns, we have seen teams in nearly every form. From elite squads and raid groups to the uncoordinated chaos of a match lobby, video games provide a glimpse into how different team dynamics work. As a video gamer, you have experienced more types of teams than you might think.

In games, teams go by many different names: Squads, Crews, Guilds, Clans, Factions, Alliances, and many more. And all these different teams serve different purposes. Some are small and tactical, while others operate on a massive scale. The names are not just for style. They reflect the different ways people organize and work together toward a goal.

One of the best-known team structures is the guild. This word comes from the Saxon term *gilden,* meaning "to pay" or "yield." Guilds first appeared in the High Middle Ages as groups of artisans and merchants who joined forces to protect their trades and support one another. Much like modern gaming guilds, these early organizations were built on cooperation and shared visions. They addressed their members' base needs and concerns like security, shelter, and food. People form groups to get more done than they ever could alone.

Teams and collaboration exist far beyond gaming. Schools, companies, and organizations all rely on structured teamwork. Class projects require students to divide tasks. Businesses depend on departments working together to deliver results. Esports teams practice for competitions with the same level of coordination as professional athletes. The patterns are the same, no matter the industry or video game.

Here is a strong definition of a team that I think follows my line of thinking:

> *"A team becomes more than just a collection of*
> *people when a strong sense of mutual commitment*
> *creates synergy, thus generating performance*
> *greater than the sum of the performance of its*
> *individual members."*
>
> - Author Unknown

Whether in a game, a workplace, or a community, the strongest teams succeed because of mutual commitment. The names and terms may change, but the foundation remains the same. Similarly, in the history of video games, developers came together to form teams to tackle more ambitious projects.

Early game development was often a solo effort or handled by small teams in which individuals wore multiple hats. As games grew in complexity, developers realized they could achieve more by combining their talents. With more artists, they could build larger and more immersive worlds. With additional engineers, they could develop new game mechanics and quality-of-life tools for players. As the industry evolved, so did the need for diverse teams with specialized roles to meet the growing demands of modern game development.

With so many ways to structure teams and define their roles in the video game industry, the real question isn't just how they form but what keeps them together. No matter the genre, scale, or purpose, every team stays intact for two fundamental reasons. We touched on some of this in "Maslow's Producer," and while psychology offers deeper theories on team dynamics, we don't need to overcomplicate it. Teams last because of:

- Shared vision

- Incentives

These two elements drive everything from small indie studios to massive AAA companies, and from casual gaming groups to professional esports organizations. Understanding them is the key to seeing why some teams thrive while others fall apart.

As discussed in so many sections so far, a shared vision is key in turning a group of individuals into a team. This vision serves as a guiding force, ensuring the group's actions are not random. Every decision has the clarity and purpose that moves the team forward to their goals. In multiplayer games, this vision is what keeps teams aligned and working toward victory. A successful team vision might be applied to clearing an entire dungeon in an MMO raid in a single night. Achieving that goal depends on every player understanding their role and how it fits into the larger strategy.

For example:

- Tanks hold the boss's attention and prevent it from attacking others.

- Healers focus on keeping the team alive, so fights do not spiral out of control.

- Damage dealers execute mechanics to weaken the boss and push the battle forward.

When players commit to the same vision, the raid runs smoothly. Everyone focuses on their responsibilities and supports the objective at hand. Without that alignment, the group will fall apart.

Now, apply this to a game studio. Imagine the team is working on a shooter with teleportation mechanics, a concept that, theoretically, hasn't been done before. Without a shared vision, everyone has a completely different idea of what the game is supposed to be. One designer thinks it should be a fast-paced arena shooter, while another imagines how useful tactical stealth mechanics could work. The engineers build mechanics that don't fit together, and the artists create assets that don't match the intended style. Instead of working toward a common goal, people are just completing tasks without clear direction.

However, shared visions at a studio level are not always about the physical project you are working on. Sometimes, it is about the people. Some teams form because they want to create a great game together, and they enjoy working together regardless of the specific project they are working on. The creative energy of a team that loves games is a powerful force. It is about gamers working with gamers. Some people care less about the product and more about who they are making it with.

Let's flip over to the other side of the coin.

Incentives *are the thing that motivates or encourages one to do something.*

Incentives shape how people stay engaged, and they go far beyond just money. A paycheck keeps the lights on, but it's not what makes someone excited about showing up every day. For most of the people I've worked with, the real incentive is creative freedom. They, and I, want the ability to shape something meaningful and original. A developer might stay at a studio because they love the people they work with, even if they could make more money elsewhere. An artist might take on extra work because they believe in the project and know players will resonate with the end results.

Others thrive on recognition, knowing their contributions are valued by their peers. Some are motivated by career growth, always looking for the next challenge that pushes their skills further. Think back to the "Maslow's Producer" section, where we explored how meeting basic needs like safety and belonging lays the foundation for motivation. Incentives work in the same way. They reinforce why people show up every day. How does this work in video games? Ask this question, "Why do you continue to play this game?"

It's easy to assume that MMO raiders are in it for the loot, but that usually isn't the full picture. Yes, some chase rare gear because they want to be stronger. Others raid because they enjoy the challenge of overcoming a boss and thrive on the fun of strategizing with a team. For others, the real pull is the social interaction and reliable commitment of logging in week after week to play with friends.

Competitive games add another layer. A ranked system or leaderboard can be an incentive, but why does climbing it matter? Is it about proving your skill in the competition and having bragging rights? It absolutely could be. Some players push for the highest rank because they love competing, just like any other sports athlete. Others do it for recognition, knowing their name on a leaderboard carries weight in the community, and they might be able to leverage that to become a video game influencer.

Even in single-player games, incentives are driving your engagement. A well-crafted story can be just as rewarding as a high rank or rare loot. Players keep going because they want to see what happens next, experience an emotional moment, or immerse themselves in a world that feels real. The incentive might be a sense of adventure or the satisfaction of completing a tough challenge.

As a video game producer, understanding what keeps your team engaged is just as important as knowing how the work gets done. Every team has different motivations, and identifying these incentives can help you align the team toward a common goal. To accomplish this, you can use a very simple approach.

Ask them directly. "Why do you continue to work here?" It's a powerful question.

It forces people to reflect on their own incentives, whether they've thought about it before or not. There's no right or wrong answer. The goal isn't to judge, but to understand what the team values and what the company offers that keeps them around. After interviewing many developers across different teams, the answers are always a mix of positive and negative:

> "I love the game and want to support it however I can."
>
> "The paycheck is far too good to leave."
>
> "I love my team and who I get to work with."
>
> "It's the only job I could get, and being in the industry is important to me."
>
> "I want my name in the credits of a video game so that I

can build a portfolio of work."

"I'm doing my best work, and it's cool to see that work making an impact."

It's important to recognize what incentives drive your team so you can work together with a clear understanding of what keeps them invested.

Full alignment isn't necessary, but the power of understanding your team's incentives can give you insight into how to work with them.

Game development teams need incentives that connect to the work. A paycheck matters. It keeps the job sustainable, but financial rewards alone won't make people care. The best teams have something beyond that. It's the spark that happens when creativity is recognized, the pride of seeing a game come to life, and knowing that the work put in made a difference.

When combined, shared visions and incentives hold teams together. One provides direction. The other reinforces commitment. When both are strong, a team does more than just complete tasks. They push further. They create something greater than the sum of their parts.

Let's dive into the fascinating world of guilds, clans, and companies to see how their cultures and policies can have a drastic impact on the shared visions and incentives for the types of people that join you.

STRUCTURE OF TEAMS AND COMPANIES

Bowser. King of the Koopas. Ruler of a vast empire built on fear and domination (*cough*, coercive power). Time and time again, he launches an assault on the Mushroom Kingdom, seizing control and kidnapping Princess Peach. His army of Koopas surges forward, marching through castles and patrolling the skies in airships in an organized, militaristic fashion.

And yet, when Mario comes to save the day and defeat him, everything collapses.

His minions scatter, his castles crumble, and the Mushroom Kingdom is restored. No second-in-command takes over. No loyal general fights to reclaim his lost territory. Without Bowser, his entire empire fades, as if it were never real to begin with.

But why?

How does one oversized, fire-breathing turtle maintain absolute control, only for his army to vanish the second he's gone? Why does Bowser's grip on power disappear instantly, while the Mushroom Kingdom continues, even when its ruler is deposed?

Look at Princess Peach's Mushroom Kingdom. There are no war factories or massive fortresses looming over the land. No robotic enforcers patrol the streets. And yet, even when Peach is kidnapped, life goes on. The Toads don't panic. The kingdom doesn't fall into chaos. So what makes the difference?

The answer lies in how authority and communications are structured. Some kingdoms are designed to survive without a leader. Others crumble the moment their ruler disappears. Bowser rules through absolute control. His minions don't think for themselves. They wait for orders, and those orders only come from him. When he's gone, everything stops.

Peach's kingdom, on the other hand, is built on something more resilient. It doesn't need a single ruler to function because power isn't centralized in one figure. The kingdom continues, no matter what happens. But what does that actually mean? What makes one structure fragile and another one strong?

In this section, we'll explore the differences between flat and hierarchical structures and how they shape communication within an organization.

A **hierarchical structure** *follows a clear chain of command, where authority moves from upper management down through multiple levels. By contrast, a* **flat structure** *minimizes manage-*

ment layers, allowing for direct interactions and faster deci-sion-making.

Each of these structures influences how information flows and how decisions are made.

In a related concept, some organizations rely on **centralized decision-making**, *where authority is concentrated at the top, ensuring consistency and control.* Others embrace **decentralized decision-making**, *which distributes authority, allowing individuals or lower-level leaders to act with greater autonomy.* These approaches shape the way organizations operate.

Before I can share with you the power of the ultimate structure, called the *Team of Teams*, we need to fully understand the interrelationship of hierarchies and decision-making.

Many organizations rely on tall hierarchical structures, like Peach's Mushroom Kingdom, where authority is distributed across multiple levels. This is a common structure that you can see modeled in several real-world scenarios, from military organizations and corporations to our raiding guilds in MMOs. Hierarchy provides order, structure, and redundancy. Roles are clearly defined. Responsibility moves downward through a chain of command. At the top, leadership makes strategic decisions. Below them, managers or officers oversee specific teams that will be executing those decisions. At the base, individuals focus on executing tasks and communicating the progress back up the chain.

A traditional hierarchy can be effective in large organizations. It ensures that decisions are made with oversight. Leaders at each level are accountable for their teams. A clear chain of command makes it easy to understand which groups exist and which individual managers manage them. It's also easier to break up the work this way. Heavy lies the crown that rests on one person's head.

However, hierarchy also comes with trade-offs. Lower levels often have little decision-making power, because multiple managers oversee different levels. Any action may require approval from a direct manager or even someone above them, which creates red tape and bottlenecks.

A flat structure eliminates traditional chains of command, allowing decisions to be made swiftly. Without a hierarchy, there's no waiting for approval or navigating through multiple levels of authority, as you can just go straight to the decision-maker. This approach is particularly effective in small groups, where speed and adaptability are paramount. Indie game studios often adopt this model, as their size necessitates flexibility. A streamlined process ensures that creativity and productivity remain unhindered in such settings. Flat structures don't have layers of supervisors or managers in tiers above you.

While flat structures can appear to have more agility, take note that they can also be fragile. Two types of situations can develop. The first happens in a truly flat organization where everyone has a voice and no one is the shot caller. The second is the opposite, where a single person makes all the decisions and can become a bottleneck.

In the latter situation, if that individual is removed or incapacitated, the organization may struggle to function effectively. This concentration of power without redundancy is only as strong as the leader is in that moment. This is similar to what we see with Bowser's kingdom. When a plumber finally wants to save the princess, he will defeat Bowser. Once Bowser is defeated, his kingdom will fall with him, as there is no one left to make decisions.

This doesn't make all flat structures a bad thing. When you play first-person games and are matched into a five-versus-five battle with others, there is no leader, making it a flat team structure. In many MOBAs, the teams battling it out do not have inherent structures and are also flat. In any game where there is no assigned role, making people responsible for specific tasks or creating different permissions within the team, it is a flat hierarchical structure. This is probably the most common structure that most gamers come across, though that is dependent on the types of games you play.

If it is so common, why does this structure work in these scenarios? In a five-on-five team shooter, the game provides inherent goals that unite a flat team. It's easy to align together if you know what you are trying to accomplish. Who are you trying to defeat, or what score are you trying to reach? This flat structure allows everyone on the team to know the goal and make individual decisions toward it without a management layer above them.

By contrast, large raiding parties in an MMO usually (but not always) have more people; having extra management makes sense, and hierarchies start to form. Most MMORPGs have guild features that assign roles and create permissions levels, allowing leaders to share responsibility for guild management. Even mobile MMO games like *Warhammer 40,000: Tacticus* have a kind of guild and team format for players to engage with. This top-down structure is becoming far more common in games.

The best guilds and companies define the roles at different levels. If you've worked in a team, you're already familiar with the way these structures function. Video game studios follow similar setups, using both hierarchical and flexible team models. Hierarchy isn't just a business concept. It has roots in the military, where leadership and chain of command play a critical role. This perspective makes it easier to see that there is no difference across games or companies, besides the names and terms being different.

Guild Roles + Hierarchy	Company Roles + Hierarchy	Military Roles + Hierarchy
Guild Leader	CEO	General
Raid Leaders	Directors	Officers
Class Leads	Team Leads	Non-Commissioned Officers (NCOs)
Guild Members	Employees	Enlisted

In both hierarchical and flat structures, there is another challenge. We need to discuss the interrelationship between these structures and how decisions are made. When every problem waits in a queue for leadership to resolve it, teams can lose momentum. They are forced to wait for the leader to make a decision rather than make adjustments on their own. This is an example of centralized decision-making, where a single leader or a small group controls most major decisions. This structure can work, especially when a strong creative vision is needed to guide a project or when a game needs to be completed quickly without external input. Many well-known game directors use this leadership style, and their teams still produce successful games in structured environments.

While teams still contribute to projects and influence decisions in this kind of structure, most choices pass through a central leader, much like a director overseeing a film. A major advantage of centralized power is efficiency. A leader with a clear vision can push projects forward without delays caused by excessive bureaucracy.

In a small team, this allows creative ideas to take shape quickly. However, as an organization grows, this structure begins to show its weaknesses.

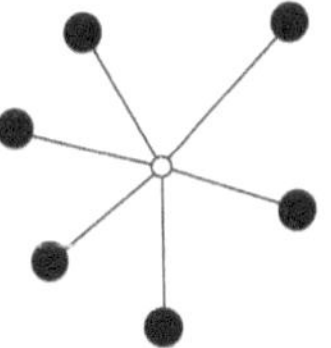

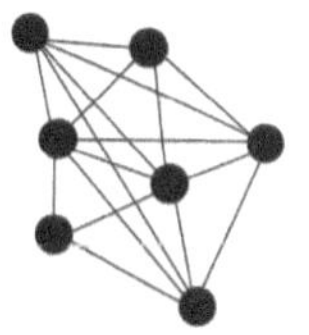

When every decision must pass through a single person or a select few, even if it's just leadership, progress will slow.

Decentralized decision-making solves this problem by spreading responsibility, creating the opportunity for decisions to be approved at multiple levels. Instead of having one person or a small group hold all authority, teams have the autonomy to make decisions aligned with the studio's shared vision. Leadership still plays a role, but rather than controlling every detail, they focus on maintaining the overall vision to ensure it's clearly understood across teams. As long as teams stay aligned with that vision, they can act independently and don't need to be micro-managed.

A real-time strategy game (RTS) where you control units is a great way to understand and play with the concept of centralized and decentralized decisions. Take games like *Command and Conquer* or *Starcraft,* where you manage and control your armies as a group of individual units. By default, the game automatically gives all of your units decentralized decision-making power to attack the enemy if they come too close. It's common sense in this game, where the goal is to defeat your enemy, and you cannot have eyes on the whole map at all times. You know that if the enemy comes near, your units have your back.

In a fully centralized system, you would have to command each unit manually, clicking on them one by one to move and attack.

Every action would require direct decision-making from you, the player. If the enemy came up and tried to attack, your units would stand there until you told them they could attack back. Centralized command is centralized to just you. This works in a game like *Sid Meier's Civilization* because it is turn-based, allowing you unlimited time to consider each of your units and make decisions for them.

However, the real world moves in real time. In the ideal video game producer situation, you should be striving for decentralized decision-making within your team. This creates an agile, effective team regardless of how the broader studio structure operates. You can implement this in your team by understanding how decisions are currently made. Find out and document the information that other people will be looking for. Who is the person who says "yes" and "no" for an upcoming feature? What are the criteria for them to make a decision? Is it data or a gut feeling? Once you know those common answers, share them with your teams so they have a protocol of options to follow. Sharing what to do in scenarios and keeping it consistent is the start of getting your team to make decentralized decisions.

Now that we've explored these structures, we can look at the ultimate format of teams, the *Team of Teams*.

This concept, introduced to me when I read General Stanley McChrystal's book of the same name, extends the benefits of decentralization across an entire organization. Instead of teams working in isolation, they operate as a connected network, all moving toward a common goal.

To make this work, he embedded members from one team into another so that groups could train and operate together. His teams in Iraq had Intelligence officers working alongside operations teams and specialists who trained directly with field units. This built trust through natural interactions and helped teams adapt in real time.

He also created a central operations hub (like a wiki) where teams could instantly share new intelligence with each other. But communication alone wasn't enough. The real shift came when McChrystal gave leaders at every level the power of decentralized decision-making. Teams could now act quickly and solve problems independently while staying aligned with the mission set by higher command.

The McChrystal Group outlines four key principles that define a team of teams:

- **Trust and Common Purpose** - A shared vision that aligns all teams.

- **Strong Team Bonds** - Relationships that create collaboration across different units.

- **Real-Time Information Sharing** - Open communication that removes delays.

- **Emphasis on Purpose over Procedure** - A focus on outcomes rather than rigid structures.

Expanding on this, I have translated this idea to both my raiding guilds and game production teams.

In large-scale raids, success depends on coordination between specialized groups. Each team has a role, but they often work in isolation. Healers focus on keeping teammates alive, while Warriors manage incoming damage from the monsters and bosses you are fighting. Damage Dealers concentrate on maximizing their attacks. Just like in real-world operations, these groups can become siloed. When something goes wrong, frustration in voice chat is inevitable.

"Why isn't this working for that team over there?"

Without seeing the challenges first-hand, it's hard to understand where the breakdown is happening. Each group follows its own system, but has little insight into the struggles of the others. This is where the Team of Teams concept changes everything. Instead of working separately, cross-training bridges the gaps.

Imagine having each Healer cross-trained with Warriors so they fully understand their class's strengths and limitations, and vice versa. Tanks, in turn, would understand what protection and callouts healers need to keep them alive. Imagine Healers cross-training with Damage dealers as well. They could learn when to request a quick heal without putting the team at risk by asking at the wrong time. This kind of cross-training builds shared understanding. Instead of feeling like separate units, every player becomes part of a larger, more adaptable force by understanding each other's roles.

When we apply this to game development teams, this is where true collaboration and decision-making apply to a creative project that requires cross-breeding. With all the multiple and diverse talent you have across all the teams, imagine them working together, all toward that same goal.

The Game Producers' Version of Team of Teams outlines four key principles:

- **Trust and Common Purpose**: We explain the shared vision of the game project until the team truly understands.

- **Strong Team Bonds**: We value creating enough time for our teams to work and learn in other departments to form bonds in understanding new systems and limitations.

- **Real-Time Information Sharing**: We have common areas and wikis where we post and share all of our latest thinking and create a space for feedback.

- **Emphasis on Purpose Over Procedure**: A focus on the outcomes of fun and working game features that align with the overall vision over the red tape of approvals.

This approach requires alignment across the entire studio.

Every leader and team member must understand why these four principles are critical if we are to make this type of structure possible. It needs a strong top-down voice, and leadership needs to set the example by cross-training with other teams and building strong working relationships. They thus establish the professionalism and structure that will shape collaboration first, before moving down to the teams. It is up to the teams themselves to ensure that other people working in this system follow the established structure and reinforce collaboration.

If teams stick together because of incentives and shared visions, teams and studios can be formed in many different ways, each with pros and cons. There is another missing ingredient that brings this whole picture together when thinking about teams. Once teams fully embrace these concepts, the focus shifts to studio culture and policies. The key is understanding that some reinforce and support these structures, while others weaken them from within. There are no right or wrong cultures and policies for teams; they come in many shapes and sizes. There are only bad ones that break the structure and foundations of teams that have been established. Let's take a deeper dive and see how culture and policies can impact team structures and dynamics.

TEAMS CULTURE AND POLICY

oblox is an amazing game for people to explore their creative outlet, and its simplicity gives players the freedom to shape their own experiences. Unlike *Minecraft*'s block-by-block building, *Roblox* empowers creators to design entire games and systems that others can play. Players join community or private servers inside these games, where they bring those creations to life. Even when playing the same game, each server can feel different, with its own culture shaped by the people inside and the rules they choose to follow.

Game creators on *Roblox* set the rules and policies by scripting the mechanics, moderation tools, and in-game expectations. They might filter certain words in chat, require uniforms in roleplay, or build systems to block griefing. Some games rely only on *Roblox's* global moderation, while others add stricter custom rules. The culture then shifts from server to server. One Brookhaven Role-Playing (RP) Server may be wholesome, with families roleplaying together, while another might be chaotic, with trolling and meme spamming. The mechanics and policies remain the same, but the culture changes entirely based on the people inside.

This is not unique to *Roblox*, or even to just player-hosted persistent worlds. All communities, in games or outside of games, have a culture that can be experienced. Some of the same games have the same culture throughout all their communities, but unique policies and vice versa. In my favorite example game, *Squad*, the community-hosted servers also have tags and signs to inform players of this. There is "Experienced Players Only" or "New Players Welcome," which provide a strong indication on the types of cultures those servers might have.

Team culture and policy are often overlooked as the reason why teams or individuals don't synergize well. The relationship between these two core elements frequently dictates how they are going to support any structure and how they will be received by the teams. A nurturing culture can spread across decentralized teams and start influencing them together, whereas a team with well-defined policies enables centralized teams to operate efficiently and uniformly without variations. A volunteer baseball league would be more relaxed in its policies than a local police station, which has stricter policies and roles. Just as you would expect a racing game to get your heart pumping in a competitive culture, you want the exact opposite in your favorite farm simulator Reddit community while talking about how to get the best results from your crops. You have experienced these at play one way or another, and more often than you might think.

To dive deeper, at the heart of this interplay is how you and your team members treat one another. Policies set boundaries and expectations, but culture breathes life into these rules. A team with a culture of trust and openness (*cough,* servant leadership) will easily align with policies that promote transparency and communication. On the other hand, a toxic culture can undermine even the most carefully designed policies. If the culture is backstabbing and fosters a dog-eat-dog world, how could individuals within that structure follow policy, let alone create it, with that kind of mentality?

Pairing a relaxed culture with strict, uncompromising policies, or a high-pressure culture with loose or unclear policies, is possible, but might be confusing for the people interacting with it. Sticking with the farm simulator analogy, imagine joining a very friendly community that wants everyone to farm together, but with extremely strict policies on what you can farm and how to farm. We need to recognize that these relationships can tell us a lot more about the communities and teams we work with. If we know it might be a high-pressure or high-stress video game, you would expect clear policies on how to operate and what to do. Think about video games like *League of Legends* and the thorough meta of how to play it. In high-competition environments, the meta, or policies, provide clarity to players. These policies were formed in high-pressure situations and built on repetitive data to identify the best option for achieving the shared goal.

Let's solidify these terms before we discuss how they relate to video game studios:

> **Team Culture:** *The shared values, behaviors, and practices that shape how team members interact, collaborate, and pursue goals.*

> **Team Policy:** *The formal rules and guidelines established to define roles, responsibilities, and expectations within a team.*

Video game studios vary widely, with many different types of cultures. Some are structured like elite esports teams, where a high-performance culture drives strict deadlines. Others resemble casual guilds focusing on work-life balance and social interactions. A studio's culture influences everything, from how team members communicate to how decisions are made.

Understanding where a studio's culture falls on this spectrum helps determine the best policies to synergize with it. A serious development team may thrive under high-performance expectations, while a creative-driven studio might need a more flexible culture that encourages innovation without rigid constraints. Consider two stereotypical studio scenarios:

> **AAA Studios** have a large team and a professional atmosphere. They use long-term planning to bring top-of-the-line gaming experiences, and profit forecasts are critical.

> **Indie Studios** usually have smaller team interactions, emphasize experimentation, and have the flexibility to take more creative risks.

There are exceptions, and this doesn't apply to all AAA or Indie Studios, but these are the very stereotypical expectations they have. Policies can generally be categorized as strict or loose. We need to understand how much flexibility they impose on the team that is working within them, to understand how strict they are.

Strict policies enforce clear, rigid rules to maintain order and predictability. These policies work well in high-stakes environments where stability and efficiency are critical. Studios with large teams, tight production cycles, and extensive stakeholder expectations tend to rely on strict policies to ensure predictability in their processes.

Strict Policy Game Studios have Scrum methodology pipelines to ensure assets move efficiently from concept to final implementation. Mandatory sprint planning meetings keep development teams aligned. Performance reviews and milestone deadlines prevent scope creep and production delays. Strict policies reduce ambiguity, ensuring every team member knows their role and expectations. However, they can also create rigidity, making it harder to adapt when unexpected challenges arise. Loose policies work well in creative environments, where innovation and exploration are driving development. Loose Policy Game Studios have open-ended brainstorming sessions where ideas evolve dynamically. They might employ flexible work hours and remote collaboration without rigid tracking. They are likely to encourage experimentation with mechanics before committing to specific features. Both of these approaches work, but which one works best in game development?

As always, there is no one-size-fits-all answer. The most effective game studios find a balance between structure and flexibility. Here is one recommended hybrid approach for game development teams:

> Use strict policies for production pipelines, deadlines, and team coordination. This ensures work progresses efficiently and keeps large teams aligned.

> Use loose policies for creative decision-making, problem-solving, and ideation. This allows designers, artists, and programmers the freedom to refine ideas organically before committing to execution.

The most successful teams adapt their policies to their culture rather than forcing culture to conform to policy. Now that we have established the importance of aligning culture and policy, it is crucial to recognize when cultural dysfunction undermines success. Even with strong policies in place, a negative or toxic culture can poison a team from within. Trust breaks down.

Engagement drops. Morale fades.

Toxicity spreads faster than most people realize, often before leadership fully understands the damage. To give a personal example, I was working at a game studio where the leadership was unempathetic with the game teams at the company. Making money and legally protecting the company were deemed to be more important than the well-being of team members.

Team members tried to change the culture, but were met with resistance, and told, "If you don't want to be here, then leave. This is how we operate." Employees who stayed but continued to fight against the rigid culture were put on a PIP (Personal Improvement Plan) to force cooperation. To you and me, this might not sound like a successful way to run a game studio. Personally, I struggled to align myself with the culture and policies they stood for.

Is this a bad thing? Yes. But did it work for them? Unfortunately, yes.

The company had stakeholders and investors, whom they were also responsible for, who provided other pressures. This was a sad reminder that some cultural styles and policies can have negative effects on people, but can nonetheless produce efficient results because the company has financial incentives or other priorities. Sometimes, they can afford to churn through employees and hire more as a sustainable model.

While this is not the case at all studios, we do need to address the negative effects of policy and culture that can be prevalent in the industry. If you think about it, video games themselves also provide a unique challenge when it comes to culture. This book has drawn comparisons between video game experiences and real-world teamwork, but not all gaming experiences are positive. Many players have witnessed or been directly affected by bad cultures in multiplayer spaces. Unlike traditional workplaces, video games exist in environments where participation is voluntary. Many online communities allow players to remain anonymous. That anonymity creates an environment where accountability is weaker, and some gamers take advantage of it.

Toxic behavior is widespread in gaming. A 2023 survey found that 75 percent of gamers in the United States, the United Kingdom, and South Korea had encountered toxic behaviors in online multiplayer games within the past year.

That number is staggering. Toxicity is not rare. It is now the normal experience for gamers online. Bad culture is not just a problem in casual online gaming. Leadership roles within gaming communities, including guild leaders, FPS teams, and esports organizations, often struggle with toxicity.

Many of these groups are competitive by nature. A team striving to be the best will sometimes justify negative behaviors in pursuit of success. In multiplayer online battle arena games, studies have shown that power dynamics and dependency between players directly influence both positive and toxic behaviors. The team structure can determine whether toxic behavior is encouraged or shut down.

I have yet to meet someone who has not encountered an overly aggressive teammate, a destructive guild leader, or an egotistical esports coach. If you have played online long enough, you have seen bad culture in action. Understanding what makes culture toxic is the first step toward preventing it. In our case, for the purposes of this book, take video game experiences and examples with a grain of salt. We are trying to look at them from a neutral perspective to understand the dynamics between players and how we can bring that experience into a potentially toxic industry culture.

How do we, as video game producers, solve this? We need to understand the limitations of policies and how they impact culture within the structures we are trying to create for our teams. Similar to our hammer and screws analogy, it just depends on the situation and the team you are working with. Sometimes it means implementing the strategies in this book, practicing servant leadership, and engaging in the culture you want to see. Sometimes, it might mean removing yourself from a toxic company because its rigid policies and toxic culture outweigh the incentives it offers for your employment with it.

STAKEHOLDERS

I stared at the screen in disbelief. Under my breath, I murmured, "This can't be happening again." No matter how much effort I put into keeping everyone happy, someone always ended up furious. This time, it was not just frustration. It was a declaration of war.

Theodore Roosevelt had taken a personal vendetta against me for the second time. I had settled a city too close to his borders, and he was making sure I paid for it. A notification flashed across the screen.

"I wanted to avoid this, you know, but your idea of peace left me no choice." I knew what was coming next. A formal denouncement. A military buildup along my border. The slow march toward war.

Expanding my empire seemed like the best decision. My people needed more land and resources to keep them satisfied. The capital had been growing, but citizens were restless. They demanded amenities, food, and luxury goods.

If I did not expand, unrest would spread through the empire. It was not greed. It was survival! But Roosevelt saw things differently. In his mind, I had overstepped my bounds. To him, I was not a ruler trying to support my people. I was an aggressor.

As I was trying to figure out how to deal with Roosevelt, another leader sent a message. Mohandas Gandhi of India had noticed the growing conflict and was not pleased. "I must object to the way you conduct your affairs. Your people are not your playthings." Gandhi had long advocated peace, but his patience was wearing thin.

If you haven't guessed the game yet, I was playing *Sid Meier's Civilization VI*, a turn-based strategy game where you guide a civilization from its infancy into becoming a major world power.

The growth and expansion of my current civilization had put me on Roosevelt's bad side, and my growing military presence had drawn Gandhi's disapproval. If I pushed too hard, I would face not just one enemy but two. I had expected Roosevelt's hostility, but Gandhi's reaction caught me off guard. He was not just watching my actions. He was judging them. The problems did not end there. My diplomatic relations with Geneva, a City-State, had begun to deteriorate. They had once been a trusted ally, providing bonuses to my research. Roosevelt's influence had changed that. The more he pressured them, the less willing they were to assist me. If they withdrew their support, my civilization's scientific progress would slow to a crawl. But not everyone was against me.

Hojo Tokimune of Japan had remained neutral throughout the

conflict. He knew about the political events between us. Unlike Roosevelt and Gandhi, he did not send threats or denounce my actions. Instead, he continued strengthening trade agreements between our nations as I was growing stronger. Our trade routes had flourished, bringing wealth and stability to both of our empires. Japan valued both military strength and cultural development. Under Hojo Tokimune's leadership, my empire benefited from a strong trade network, which made us natural allies.

Roosevelt and Gandhi attempted to isolate me from any other leader's support. Losing his support would not only jeopardize our alliances but also threaten the prosperity of my empire, as Japan's military and cultural prowess were crucial for maintaining balance and power in the region.

This left me with a choice. Roosevelt would escalate the conflict if I doubled down and defended my expansion. But if I built up my army, Gandhi would see me as a warmonger. If I neglected my trade, Tokimune might reconsider his loyalty. Every decision had consequences. Expanding my empire had kept my people happy, but strengthened my rival's dislike for me. If I made another move, someone would be pleased, and someone else would be furious. The problem was figuring out who would be which. At that moment, I discovered that the game wasn't solely about land or military might. It was really about managing the relationships with the people and leaders surrounding me.

Roosevelt was a protector of his continent and would not tolerate expansion near his borders. Gandhi despised war and would not hesitate to turn against me if I pushed too hard. Geneva wanted stability and had to choose between loyalty to me and bending to Roosevelt's pressure. Hojo Tokimune, on the other hand, saw the value of our partnership. He could be the key to keeping my civilization strong if I did not act recklessly.

None of them cared about what I wanted. They all had their own agendas.

In game development, we call these groups stakeholders. They are the people who have a vested interest in what happens next. They can be any person involved in the project directly or indirectly, with authority or without authority.

Stakeholders all have different needs and desires. Some want stability, others want progress, and some just want to take advantage of a situation when the time is right. The trick is not avoiding conflict. It is learning how to mitigate negative consequences.

Stakeholder management is crucial for any project. The ultimate goal is to keep track of what each stakeholder wants, understand how their needs align with the project, and ensure everyone's expectations stay aligned. To do this effectively, we need to:

1. Identify the different types of stakeholders involved in the project.

2. Determine the best ways to work with these stakeholders.

3. Categorize these stakeholders based on their interests and power to prioritize their needs.

Now, let's walk through this process step by step.

Step 1: Identifying Stakeholders

Stakeholders *are individuals or groups with an interest in the project.* They can either influence or be affected by the project. Their roles can range from being actively involved in decision-making to simply being impacted by the final outcomes.

Stakeholders can come in different forms, such as:

Direct Team Members: These are the people actively working on the project: designers, engineers, artists, and anyone contributing to the hands-on creation of the project.

Indirect Team Members: Support teams, such as marketing, HR, or operations, who may not be directly involved in the development process but still influence or are affected by the project.

External Parties: These can be investors, clients, partners, or collaborators who have a vested interest in the project's success.

End Users: The ultimate stakeholders are the people or organizations that will use or consume the product. In video games, that is the Player.

Step 2: Determine the best ways to work with these stakeholders

Once you've identified your stakeholders, the next step is determining how to work with them. This step is highly dependent on the stakeholder and the relationship you want to have with them. A simple tool for implementing this is called the **4 C's.** These four steps are easy to remember and can help you manage these relationships effectively.

Communicate: Open, transparent communication is key.

Each stakeholder has different communication preferences, so setting up clear communication standards for updates is important. Stakeholders might need different levels of detail in their reports. Identifying what works and doesn't work for them is important. Regular, tailored communication helps prevent misunderstandings and keeps everyone aligned.

Consult: Engage with stakeholders early in the process to understand their needs and expectations.

Consulting helps set clear goals, identify potential challenges, and align everyone's understanding of the project from the start. It's as easy as asking them direct questions to get direct answers. Get their opinion. Ask them how they feel about the project.

Collaborate: Encourage active participation.

Collaboration means working together on key decisions, brainstorming ideas, and getting input from stakeholders. Involving them in decision-making will improve the project and help build trust and investment in the outcome. The best way to get answers besides consulting is getting them to collaborate to see their level of interest and expectations.

Co-Create: This goes a step further, especially with external stakeholders.

Co-creation involves actively involving them in the development process, gathering their ideas, and using their input to shape the project. When stakeholders feel they've helped shape the project, they're more likely to support it throughout its lifecycle and understand the constraints and limitations.

Step 3: Stakeholder Categorization (Stakeholder Analysis)

With the 4 C's in place, the next important step is to categorize your stakeholders. By categorizing stakeholders based on their power and interest in the project, you can prioritize your efforts and ensure you're meeting the needs of the most influential players.

Stakeholder Analysis typically uses a grid to assess where each stakeholder falls:

Manage Closely

Stakeholders with high influence and high power in your projects are the most important to keep an eye on. They need to be managed closely, involved in decisions, and kept updated at all times.

Keep Satisfied

These stakeholders have the ability to impact the project with their high power but are less concerned with the details. It's important to keep them satisfied by providing periodic updates without overwhelming them with unnecessary details.

Keep Informed

These stakeholders are passionate about the project, but don't hold much power. They should be kept informed and engaged, as their feedback can be valuable in shaping certain aspects of the project.

Monitor

These stakeholders have little influence and minimal concern about the project. While it's still important to keep an eye on them, they require minimal effort in terms of engagement.

By categorizing stakeholders this way, you can make sure that you spend enough time and energy with each stakeholder as needed. You can focus your energy on those who will significantly impact the project's success and ensure their needs are addressed accordingly.

If we jump back to my

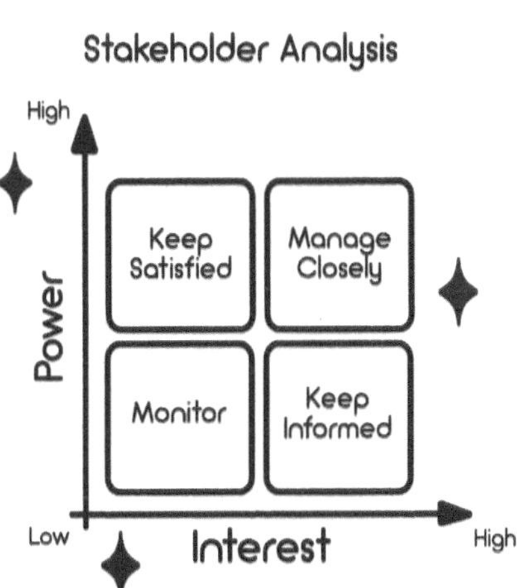

experience in *Civilization VI,* Theodore Roosevelt serves as a high-power, high-interest stakeholder. His proximity to my expanding borders made him deeply invested in my actions.

This placed him in the "Manage Closely" category, a fact I overlooked, leading to a diplomatic disaster. By failing to consider Roosevelt's territorial concerns and aggressive nature, I set the stage for conflict.

It's important not to have blinders on, though, as Roosevelt wasn't the only stakeholder. Other world leaders, each with their own unique priorities, represented the different types of stakeholders we needed to account for: Gandhi's objections to my expansion were a direct result of his commitment to peace, positioning him in the "High Power, High Interest" category, though his approach was less direct than Roosevelt's. Also, Geneva was another critical stakeholder, reflecting "Keep Satisfied" as they had interests in stability.

In games like *Civilization VI,* managing stakeholders is a perfect analogy to being a video game producer who has to manage the stakeholders at a game studio. Finding out who the stakeholders are on your project should be a high priority when joining a team. Ask for any documentation or organization charts to see who the important and relevant people are within the organization. Ask the team directly, "Who are the external parties that are known to us?" If no one has this written down, be a good producer and document it to share with the rest of the teams so they know, too.

Recognizing these dynamics early and addressing them effectively is key to avoiding conflict and ensuring project success. Understanding stakeholder analysis helps navigate these relationships and ensures that each decision aligns with the project's broader objectives.

Now that we have explored the full scope of stakeholders and their impact, it is time to focus on the direct team members. These are the people actively working on the project. Designers, Engineers, and Artists contribute to the hands-on creation of the game. Their decisions shape every aspect of production. They work within the vision set by leadership, while solving the daily challenges of development.

VIDEO GAME CLASS STRUCTURES, ROLES, SPECIALTIES

Pokémon has many lessons for us all, and playing *Pokémon Red and Blue* on the Nintendo Game Boy was no exception. I had two brothers, so the three of us all got the game Pokémon, and made a deal to pick different starters. My oldest brother got Charmander. I'm the middle brother, so I chose Squirtle. My younger brother picked Bulbasaur.

I fell in love with Squirtle. I just knew I was a water-type Pokémon user. You probably know this, but Squirtle's final evolution is Blastoise. He has a giant water cannon on his back and looks like a bouncer at the club. In the animated TV show, there was also the Squirtle Squad, a group of Squirtles with sunglasses, which was the pinnacle of cool at the time when that was aired on TV in 1998. Squirtle was my guy.

My brothers and I were all competitive, so of course, we wanted to see who had the best Pokémon team in the house. Naturally, we locked ourselves in our rooms, playing nonstop for the whole weekend. We were leveling up to the point where we could try to fight each other in-game at the Colosseum to see who could have the strongest team.

I was determined to stick with the specialization of water-type Pokémon so they would all be the same as Squirtle. Once my team had defeated all the in-game trainers and NPCs, I capitalized on the moment. I ran across the hallway, kicked open my older brother's door, and shouted, "DUEL ME!" My older brother wasn't one to step away from challenges. But I could see he had some doubt, and he started making excuses before the battle even began. He said that his team was focused on trying to do a specific thing, and he wasn't trying to build a dueling team. When I saw his Pokémon line-up, it all made sense.

In Pokémon, there is a combat mechanic for strengths and weaknesses so that certain types can do more damage to others. Fire was weak to water. My brother, staying loyal to Charmander and the fire-type specialization, built an all fire-based team. My entire team was all water-type Pokémon.

My older brother stood no chance. My water-type team destroyed his fire-type team. A roar of success erupted from me. He immediately tried to downplay my success as a technicality, but I ignored it. I was now the dominant brother in the household.

After taking down the older brother, I did what any middle brother would do next. I had to have no challengers to this throne. I kicked down my little brother's door and shouted, "DUEL ME!" Smaller than me, he might have been, but he grinned with confidence instead of shaking in his boots. That threw me off at first. What was going on? In a moment of clarity, I suddenly realized my mistake and foresaw the outcome of this duel. I had picked all water-types. My youngest brother had picked all grass-types. Water-type was weak against grass-type. I stood no chance.

Just seconds after my team was annihilated, there was the roar of success from my younger brother, and my eyes rolled. Naturally, he did what any younger brother would do. He ran over to my older brother's room, kicked open his door, and shouted, "DUEL ME!" I'm not sure he had the foresight to realize that his grass-types would be weak against fire-types.

Meanwhile, I went back to the game to diversify my team before attempting another duel.

In games, class roles highlight both strengths and weaknesses. Many of these systems were shaped by early role-playing games. The "Holy Trinity" of an RPG group are Tanks, Healers, and Damage Dealers, which create a synergy that covers and complements each role's strengths and weaknesses. While more prominent in role-playing games, this structure has now become a staple across many genres.

But why is it a trinity? Why not have a team of all tanks? Or a team of wizards! Because each role also has limitations. A warrior tank might have high health points, but is probably also limited to short-range combat with a sword and shield. A wizard might be weaker, with fewer health points, but they can fight and cast spells that do great damage from a distance.

These classes or specializations have strengths and weaknesses individually. When we look at our weaknesses, we can supplement them by introducing another type of character to help us in that area. It's called a "trinity" to show the connection among those three roles and how they become stronger when all three are present. Shooting games used to be very basic. There were no class roles or specializations. Early titles like *Doom* and *Wolfenstein 3D* were straightforward first-person shooters, where the hero had only a gun and bullets to attack enemies directly in front of them.

As online multiplayer and live service games evolved, we saw this shift within the FPS genre to also embrace the design concept of giving players more specializations. Modern shooting games have introduced Scouts (or Snipers), Assault (Close combat), Medics (Healers), and Engineers (Anti-tank). Each class has specialties that synergize with their weapons. We now have a genre called "Hero Shooters," which give each player customized classes with abilities instead of different weapon types. We are continuing to see more genres adopt specializations in their own way, because diverse team play in games is just fun. When you play different roles, they usually synergize with each other, and people see the value. The saying that a team should be well-rounded is apt.

In the Pokémon story, it's possible to stick to one type of elemental Pokémon, as all three of us did, but we needed to understand our limitations before we each gallantly charged into each other's rooms, overestimating our capabilities.

Game studios have a vast amount of talent, but most of the general roles you will find at every studio (excluding producers) fall within these main categories:

> **Designers** focus on how the game plays.
>
> **Engineers** handle the technical side.
>
> **Artists** create the visuals.
>
> **Quality Assurance (QA)** ensures the game functions as intended.

Teams usually start with a generalist position within these categories, especially if they are smaller.

However, each of these roles can evolve into more specialized positions. As a Pokémon analogy, just as Pokémon can evolve and gain new abilities, generalist roles in game development can grow into specialized paths as well.

Understanding how each role contributes to the whole is critical for collaboration. Large teams are more likely to have specialists who refine specific aspects of the game.

Every team, no matter its size, works best when roles are clearly defined and responsibilities are understood. As a video game producer, the more familiar you are with the roles you will encounter, the stronger your ability to manage them effectively. Just like knowing which Pokémon have strengths and weaknesses against others, understanding these roles will help you build a well-rounded team suited for your needs.

As a video game producer, you need to ensure you understand the different specializations of the game developers on your team. Do not make the mistake of thinking your game developers are Pokémon with strict rules and abilities. We are talking about human beings, who are unique and bring their own take on all of these roles.

My recommendation when joining any team as a new producer is to immediately carve out time to meet with your team members. Here are the questions you should consider asking during these conversations, but craft them however you want:

What is your role called?

What work do you handle?

What work would you not handle, and why?

What could I do today to make your work easier?

Let's take a look at the most common game development roles, a brief list of their specializations, and how they have evolved.

The Role of a Designer

The designer is the creative architect of a video game. They shape how players interact with the world. They define the mechanics, systems, and overall story, ensuring everything works together to create an engaging game.

How the Role Classically Functions

Early designers handled broad aspects of development. They would be involved in all elements of the design since they were smaller and straightforward. As genres advanced, certain systems required further expertise, like world design or new specific systems to handle new technology.

How the Role Has Evolved

As games became more complex, designers specialized into roles such as:

- **World Designer:** Builds immersive settings and lore.

- **Systems Designer:** Develops rules and mechanics for balance and engagement.

- **Content Designer:** Creates missions, characters, and in-game content.

- **Narrative Designer:** Writes stories, dialogue, and lore delivery methods.

- **Level Designer:** Crafts environments that challenge and guide players.

The Role of an Engineer

Engineers are the technical backbone of game development. They write the code that powers the game. They take their own design concepts, as well as those of other team members, and create functional experiences. Their work ensures the game runs smoothly and remains responsive across any platform the game is sold on.

How the Role Classically Functions

Early engineers handled all aspects of coding. They built core systems, AI behaviors, and all the UI you interact with. As areas grew more complex, the need for more systems grew, and these specialized mechanics needed more code, so engineers started to specialize in those areas as well.

How the Role Has Evolved

As games grew in complexity, Engineers specialized in areas such as:

- **Gameplay Developer:** Implements mechanics and player interactions.

- **AI Developer:** Creates intelligent NPC behaviors and decision-making.

- **Graphics Developer:** Optimizes rendering and visual performance.

- **Tools Developer:** Builds tools and frameworks for other team members in their engine.

- **Network Developer:** Manages online gameplay, matchmaking, and player data.

The Role of an Artist

Artists create a game's visuals. They design the characters, create lush environments for worlds, and add the right amount of special effects. It is all the smooth animations that make the game feel real. By blending creativity and technical skill, artists ensure the game's visuals represent the core vision of the game.

How the Role Classically Functions

Early game artists were generalists, handling most visual aspects. They created 2D illustrations, modeled characters, and animated movements. In smaller teams, one artist worked on everything from UI to environments, meaning they needed versatility. As complexity grew, so did the specializations that consistently pushed the boundaries of games.

How the Role Has Evolved

Modern development has led to specialized art roles such as:

- **Concept Artist:** Defines the initial look and style of the game.

- **3D Modeler:** Creates detailed 3D characters, vehicles, and objects.

- **Texture Artist:** Adds realism through textures and materials.

- **Environment Artist:** Builds immersive settings and landscapes.

- **Animator:** Brings characters and objects to life with movement.

- **UI/UX Artist:** Creates user-friendly and visually appealing interfaces.

The Role of a Tester (Quality Assurance)

QA testers ensure that a game is playable and bug-free for everyone. They identify bugs, glitches, and inconsistencies that might ruin the players' experience and work with engineers and designers to ensure they get fixed before players find them.

How the Role Classically Functions

QA was once a final checkpoint in development. Testers played through the game, documenting issues like crashes, broken mechanics, and performance problems under tight deadlines. It's not just a role where you are playing video games every day; it's a highly technical craft that is specialized in specific types of tests that you might not have imagined.

How the Role Has Evolved

Modern QA is a continuous process with specialized roles:

- **Functional Tester:** Ensures game mechanics work correctly.

- **Compatibility Tester:** Checks performance across platforms and devices.

- **Performance Tester:** Focuses on frame rates, load times, and optimization.

- **Localization Tester:** Verifies translations, voice-overs, and cultural accuracy.

- **Compliance Tester:** Ensures the game meets platform certification standards.

- **Automated Test Engineer:** Develops scripts to streamline bug detection.

The Role of a Hybrid Team Member

Hybrid roles combine skills from multiple areas of game development. These team members connect disciplines, improving collaboration and adaptability.

How the Role Classically Functions

In small studios or early development, hybrid roles emerged out of necessity. Engineers who could code and design, or artists who could animate, helped teams cover more ground with fewer people.

How the Role Has Evolved

Today, hybrid roles are more structured and valued. Teams intentionally recruit individuals who can operate across disciplines:

- **DevOps:** Manages game builds, deployment pipelines, and server infrastructure, to ensure smooth development and live operations.

- **Technical Artist:** Bridges art and engineering by optimizing or creating new assets, shaders, and visual effects.

- **Audio Designer:** Creates sound effects, music, and voiceovers to enhance immersion and storytelling.

- **MoCap Artist:** Captures movement for lifelike character animations using motion capture technology.

- **Product Manager:** Uses data analysis and player feedback to guide development and business decisions.

It's important to understand that every role listed, from Engineers, Artists, to these hybrid roles, is going to continue to evolve, and some of these roles might already be out of date.

Sometimes the role stays the same, but different teams or companies just call them something else. The key takeaway is that these roles should work together. You want a diverse team that can contribute to many different aspects of the game. We want to make sure we have a solid and clean code base that engineers can work in. We want the art and animation in our games to be fine-tuned and polished. Having audio specialists come in to make sure that, with every swing of your sword, you can hear the swift hiss of the blade cutting through the air. Lastly, you want individuals who can test and ensure that when players get your game in their hands, it has been tested and works.

As mentioned earlier, producers share the same responsibilities as traditional Project Managers, and a big portion of those responsibilities is to see projects or tasks from start to finish. The start-to-finish life cycle of projects and tasks involves team members and roles interacting at different times, collaborating and contributing until the project is finished. It is important to understand how these different, diverse roles should come together and work through the different phases in the life-cycle of the project. The next section explains how to apply everything we have learned so far from our previous lessons to manage projects or tasks with any type of team we might need to work with.

Projects - Large Scale Coordination

I sat there open-mouthed in my friend Mark's room, as I watched him play *Battlefield 1942*. "This is incredible! How are all these people playing at the same time? Wait, you can also control vehicles and use them against other players?" I said astonished by the technology.

The year was 2002, and the sheer scale of the game left me speechless. There were 64 players fighting at once, capturing objectives, driving armored vehicles, and piloting planes that could let you drop bombs from the skies. It was a level of fun at a massive scale like nothing I had experienced before.

Seeing so many players engaged in real-time combat was astonishing, especially given the limitations of gaming technology at the time. Massive multiplayer experiences had existed before, in games like *Ultima Online* (1997) and *EverQuest* (1999), but those were MMORPGs. They were slower and more methodical, built for large worlds, with low graphics to maintain performance.

At the time, large-scale battles were mostly found in MMO raiding guilds. Joining one required an application process similar to getting a job, with specific requirements that players had to meet. This made it difficult for many gamers to access those experiences, since those games unintentionally created a barrier to entry. As technology advanced and internet speeds improved, matchmaking evolved to automatically place players into massive servers. With pre-created teams ready from the start of the match, large-scale battles became more accessible to the average gamer.

That night at Mark's house, the world of gaming was shifting, forging digital teams in an unprecedented way, hinting at a future none of us could yet fully see. It was more than just an exciting, new online video game.

A few years later, in 2004, *World of Warcraft* launched, bringing MMO raiding into the mainstream gaming experience. Large-scale cooperative gameplay became more accessible, and players who had never experienced raiding before joined guilds for the first time. Unlike its predecessors of *EverQuest and Ultima Online*, there were no excessive barriers and challenges to form raids with other players.

Developers embraced this trend by creating more content and new challenges that needed coordination. At the same time, streaming platforms like Twitch and YouTube were also growing, showcasing this new content to a broader audience. This accessibility gave players additional help. Gamers who once had trouble finding guides could now watch videos breaking down strategies, raid leadership, and team coordination in real time.

As these evolved, the genre of large-scale coordination games took shape. Patterns emerged from players to address challenges that closely aligned with the principles of project management. Teams working toward their in-game visions were, in reality, setting up "projects."

A **project** *is a system for organizing work, allocating resources, and managing time to reach a planned outcome.*

I'll be clear with my point up front. Everything you aim to accomplish in a video game, whether online or solo, is a goal that can be structured like a project. Each planned outcome is the result of setting objectives and working toward them. Video games give you the opportunity to take on projects whenever you play a game.

For these game genres, the standard objectives are:

- **MMO Raiding**: Defeat the boss at the end of the dungeon.

- **Shooting Games**: Eliminate enemies and secure objectives.

Since any outcome can follow a structured system approach, applying project management principles as a Raid Leader or Squad Leader can help achieve them more effectively, and you are likely already doing it. Let's take a look at that structured system approach.

All projects have an end outcome. The project life cycle consists of the phases a project goes through from *inception to completion.*

The same framework applies to any type of project across all industries and games.

1. **Initiation**: Identify the project's goals.

2. **Planning**: Make a plan

3. **Executing**: Do the plan

4. **Monitoring & Controlling**: Review and adjust the plan as needed.

5. **Closing**: Finish the work and achieve the project goals.

Sticking with the raiding example, let me show you how this framework can be very similar to the experiences you already have. Also, this is a very practical chapter that draws on the information we have explored in all the previous chapters, with significant overlap. I will focus on the most prominent lessons for each part of this framework.

Initiation (Previous lessons: *Visions + Shared Visions*)

- Identify the Raid's Vision/Goal: Defeat the boss at the end of the dungeon.

The players align on the vision or goal, ensuring everyone understands the purpose of the encounter and their role in it. It's a straightforward goal the players can understand: simply defeat a specific boss at the end of the dungeon.

Planning (Previous lessons: *Production Taskmaster*)

1. **What needs to be done?** Need to complete a dungeon raid that has three mini-bosses and one main boss that have unique mechanics and abilities for us to mitigate.

2. **Why are we doing it?** The raid bosses drop treasures and rewards (loot) that are considered the best in the game.

3. **Who needs to do it?** Finding out how many people we need in certain classes (i.e, tanks, healers, and

damage dealers) while also ensuring a designated raid leader keeps track of execution and adjustments.

4. **How long should each step take?** With estimates and data from previous experiences, we can estimate the time our plan will take.

Executing (Previous lessons: *Leadership + Human System Building*)

- The team follows the plan, executing their role responsibilities.

The production taskmaster ensures successful methods are documented and refined to create a structured, repeatable system for future encounters.

Monitoring & Controlling (Previous lessons: *Speedrunning*)

- The team treats every attempt as a learning opportunity.

Wipes are reviewed and analyzed in the same way a speedrunner re-watches a failed run. We need to identify inefficiencies and adjust strategies as needed to stay on course.

Closing (Previous lessons: *Team Culture + Policy*)

- Once the boss is defeated, loot is distributed fairly, based on agreed policies.

The team recognizes effort and contributions, reinforcing positive behaviors and maintaining long-term motivation.

Key takeaways from the raid are documented and shared in the central hub, bulletin board, or wiki so we can reference them for future challenges.

If this generally makes sense, let's take the same structure and apply it to how it works in video game development. There are many ways to do this, but below is a straightforward way to apply it to any project or task. I've added a layer of questions to ask at each stage. In doing so, you can understand what you need to do in order to move past that phase.

Initiation (Previous lessons: *Visions + Shared Visions*)

Whenever we start a project, whether it's developing a game or setting out on an in-game quest, we need to establish its purpose and objectives.

Questions to ask:

- Why are we doing this?

- What are we trying to achieve?

- Who would be involved in this?

In video games, just as we choose to invest our time in playing them, development teams must decide whether they are committed to seeing a project through. This is the moment when dedication is established and the vision is set in motion.

Here's what we need to define:

- **The Project Goal** - Clearly articulate what the project aims to achieve and how it aligns with the vision for the game. A strong vision will ensure that the entire development team moves in sync toward a common goal.

    ◊ Lesson Callback - Think of the video game design pillars.

- **The Stakeholders** - Identify all parties impacted and involved in the project. Engage them early to align expectations and establish clear communication channels, ensuring they remain informed throughout development (i.e., 4Cs).

Planning (Previous lessons: *Production Taskmaster*)

Once we've decided to move forward with a project, whether it's developing a game or creating a new feature, the next step is to map out exactly how we're going to achieve it.

Questions to ask:

- What do we need to do?

- What resources and time will it take?

- What risks should we prepare for?

This is where we break down the steps, set expectations, and make sure everyone understands their role. Planning turns good intentions into action, ensuring strategies become reality.

Here's what we need to define:

- **Game Design Document (GDD)** - A comprehensive document that outlines the vision, mechanics, features, gameplay loops, narrative, art style, and overall player experience of a video game.

- **Technical Design Document (TDD)** - A comprehensive document, similiar to GDD, but details the technical implementation plan for a game's features based off the GDD's plan.

- **The Requirements (Scope)** - The list of deliverables that are needed to complete the project.

  The scope must remain clear from the start, as it defines exactly what features are necessary for the project's success. The GDD and TDD are the two documents that should help us understand the full scope of work.

- **The Timeline** - Setting milestones and deadlines to track progress and ensure timely completion based on the estimations from the scope.

When we combine timelines and tasks on a roadmap, we are creating a Gantt chart. A Gantt chart is a visual timeline that shows what tasks need to be done, when they start and end, and how they overlap. It helps teams stay organized by clearly laying out the schedule for a project.

- **The Budget** - Estimating the time and resources necessary to meet the project's scope and timeline.

  Game production is full of unexpected costs, from tool licensing to post-launch maintenance. The budget must account for flexibility while ensuring that payroll, software, and production costs remain under control.

  You should never do the planning solo; this step requires the team's assistance so they can help verify the scope and plans.

  Recall back to our previous chapter on being the production taskmaster. This role emphasizes that a video game producer must ensure all tasks are mapped out in a way that allows for ongoing tracking, so the right work is done at the right time.

Executing (Previous lessons: *Leadership + Human System Building*)

Once the plan is in place, it's time to put it into action. At this stage, we should have a general understanding of the scope of work and how long it will take.

Questions to ask:

- Are the plans and tasks accessible for the team?

- Have we set up proper kickoff meetings?

- Were all the previous concerns or questions addressed?

Now we need to get the team to start working; the three activities that we need to start are:

- **Task Execution** - Just like the leveling and farming guides, we need to make sure the team has the steps and checklists they need to complete.

- **Communication** - Make sure the tools you are using for communication (like Slack or Discord) are consistent and reliable.

- **Problem Resolution** - Have a culture that allows for problems to escalate, but also has tools for resolution so that we can fix them before they delay the work too far.

Bonus: Tips & Tricks for this Phase

Callouts *are concise, real-time verbal instructions or alerts used to direct a team during critical moments.* They ensure everyone has the same situational awareness and knows what to focus on without lengthy explanations. They are similar to slang, as they're shorthand with shared understandings among the people using them.

The key to effective callouts is keeping them short and clear. They should deliver the necessary information as quickly as possible so that the team can act immediately.

For video game producers, callouts can also take the form of status updates from team members. These are quick, straightforward statements that communicate progress, identify issues, or provide clarity on current tasks.

Examples of status update callouts include:

- "I'm on track." - A simple confirmation that tasks are proceeding as planned.

- "It's currently still in progress." - This indicates that

work is ongoing and there are no immediate issues.

- "I'm blocked." - Flags a problem or dependency that must be resolved in order to move forward.

Monitoring & Controlling (Previous lessons: *Speedrunning*)

Keeping everything on track as the project progresses is essential if we want to complete it on time. This phase involves monitoring the project's progress closely and making adjustments as needed. We want to make sure we hit the dates in our most recent plans.

Questions to ask:

- Are we on track?

- What's working?

- What's not working?

- What needs to change?

Here's what we need to define:

- **Progress Tracking** - Regularly checking in on tasks and milestones to make sure everything stays aligned with the plan.

  It's more than just marking tasks as complete, as discussed in the Speedrunning lesson. Tracking progress means using data to make smart decisions, adjusting priorities when needed, and keeping the team working efficiently.

- **Change Management** - Adjusting plans and strategies to handle unexpected challenges or new opportunities

Change management is a straightforward process whereby we track any adjustments and clearly communicate them to the team. We avoid making changes without a system that keeps everyone informed and aligned.

- **Quality Assurance** - Making sure everything we produce meets our standards and aligns with the overall goal.

Quality assurance isn't just a final pass at the end. It's something we continuously do throughout development to keep quality high and catch issues early, so we don't get hit with bigger delays later.

Closing (Previous lessons: *Team Culture + Policy*)

Once we've completed the video game and reached the end of its project lifecycle, it's time to officially close things out.

This phase is about finishing up any remaining tasks, reviewing how successful we were, capturing key lessons learned, and archiving everything clearly so we can easily reference it during future projects.

Questions to ask:

- Did we achieve our goals?

- What did we learn?

- How do we celebrate the effort?

In video games, this means looking at the end scores and results, then taking a moment to appreciate them. When the dust settles and rewards are handed out, how well did we do? It's the moment we look back at what went well, and what didn't, then make sure our team is ready for whatever comes next.

Here's what we focus on:

- **Final Deliverables** - Making sure we've achieved everything we set out to do and that our game's goals are fully met.

  Our deliverables should be thoroughly verified so we're not left with last-minute issues or unresolved problems.

- **Knowledge Transfer** - Capturing the lessons we learned, documenting best practices, and archiving resources clearly.

  Doing this well means future teams can learn from our experiences, avoid repeating our mistakes, and get better each time.

- **Celebration & Reflection** - Recognizing the team's effort and taking a moment to think about what we accomplished together.

  Celebrating boosts morale, builds stronger relationships, and reminds everyone they're valued as we prepare for the next big challenge.

The video game producer ensures the final product meets quality expectations, delivers the game to players, and reflects on the development process. They host a post-mortem meeting (recall back to *Scrum*) to document lessons learned and celebrate the team's hard work with a launch party or other recognition.

And that's it, you've done it! By the end of the Closing phase, you are now officially a producer. If you are able to see a project or task from start to finish, you did your actual job. Welcome to the club of Video Game Producers.

There are only two more sections left in Part Two that will discuss Team Morale and what to be aware of when managing teams and getting projects and tasks done. Understanding how a project lifecycle functions is critical if you want to be a video game producer in this industry. With all the human system-building we are doing on a team, we need to make sure we understand the team's limitations. So, we are going to take a closer look at team morale.

Finally, we are going to wrap up with what it means to have a Ranked versus Casual mindset and how that applies to our personal lives and careers.

Team Morale

It's November 2004, and my foot is pressing the pedal to the metal in my 1964 Chevy, causing its engine to roar as I speed down the freeway. I've just ditched high school for the first time, and I am now racing to the next town over because they have a *Best Buy* store. I had pre-ordered the sequel to my favorite game, *EverQuest 2*, and I wanted to be first in line to get my copy. To my surprise, however, there was no line, but that is besides the point. I got my copy and immediately rushed back home.

My guildmates all wanted to start a new guild on launch day, and we were so excited to play together again in a new game. Since I had ditched school on a Thursday, the timing was perfect. I had a "sick day" that Friday, which basically gave me ninety-six hours of gaming with my friends. We got to level up our new characters together, without sleeping and living on Chinese takeout and Red Bull energy drinks. Were we happy? Sure, for a bit. Did all the bad food and drinks start to upset our stomachs? Of course. Is this kind of weekend binge gaming actually fun or even a good idea? Only the people doing it can say. I don't regret that particular instance, but I wouldn't do it again.

How about you? What's your record for marathon game-playing? How long have you played video games in one sitting? Have you ever started in the morning and kept going until you could barely keep your eyes open? Maybe you stayed up through the night and only realized the time once the sun was already rising. These marathon sessions might feel exciting in the moment, but they come at a cost. You finish exhausted and distracted, and have a tough time bouncing back.

The same principle applies when working on projects. You are probably aware that video game development is infamous for **crunch**, *where teams push beyond normal working hours.* According to the International Game Developers Association's (IGDA) 2023 Developer Satisfaction Survey, conducted in partnership with Western University, crunch remains a significant issue in the video game industry.

The survey found that "28% of respondents reported that their job involved crunch time," although this represented a slight decrease from previous years. Additionally, among those experiencing crunch, "63% of employees, 64% of freelancers, and 75% of the self-employed had crunched more than twice in the past two years." Many game developers, particularly freelancers, reported that "crunch or long hours were expected as a normal part of their job."[10]

---

10   International Game Developers Association. (2023). *Developer Satisfaction Survey.* Retrieved January 30, 2025.

This sounds like just an unfortunate reality of working in this industry, but as producers, we have to take a closer look at how it affects our team. Maslow's hierarchy of needs highlights the importance of meeting basic requirements and our team's needs. Without proper rest and a sense of security, a team's performance suffers. When these needs are ignored, productivity and quality take a hit. You are going to be stressed if you feel like you are not getting enough sleep or food. And you are going to be stressed if you feel like your job (security) might be at risk, given the pressure to get work done.

When crunch happens, some stay late into the night while others sacrifice weekends just to keep up with deadlines. For many, crunch feels like grinding in an RPG. The same tasks are repeated with the hope that progress will follow. But, just like in games, too much grinding wears people down. Exhaustion sets in, motivation drops, and the team's creative spark fades. As a video game producer, keeping an eye on team morale is a key responsibility.

Pay attention to when efficiency drops or mistakes increase, as these are early signs of burnout and shouldn't be ignored. If energy feels low across the team, it's a sign that you need to step in. Protecting the well-being of the people who bring your project to life matters just as much as maintaining productivity. Your leadership sets the tone!

Encouraging breaks and keeping an eye on team energy helps maintain a productive pace. Show that you value rest by leading through action. Step away when needed, maintain balance, and avoid creating a culture where long hours seem the only path to success. If producers ignore healthy values, the team follows that example. If you are stressed and working late every night, the entire team will feel that this is now the expectation, not a last resort.

There are many techniques you can use to keep team morale high, but once again, the most effective method is *simply checking in* and asking the team directly. A direct question gets a direct answer. If the team has built trust with you and believes in the servant leadership principles, you will get an honest response.

Try asking:

- "Just checking in. How are you feeling today?"

- "Do you need anything?"

There is also a sense of pride that we all feel, especially as artists, designers, and developers. Even if you have built a safe place of trust with the servant leadership principles, asking follow-up questions can be insightful in gauging how your team really feels:

- "Are you confident in what you're working on?"

- "Is there anything I can clarify, or can I get anyone else to help clarify something?"

As simple as it is, asking questions and understanding what your team is thinking and feeling through their words is key. I cannot stress enough that this is not possible if the values and trust of servant leadership aren't already in place. If your team does not trust you to have their back, you can't expect them to be open with you. When you ask these types of questions, they might lie to you and not give you a direct or truthful answer.

During my time on *Rocket League,* we had a critical update that was needed to help protect our players' privacy. We had a tight deadline and a ton of development work, which would require late nights and weekend days from our engineers. It might feel kind of hopeless to be a producer in that type of scenario, because your options are very limited and you have no choice but to get the work done. That being said, I dedicated myself to being part of every meeting our engineers were in, so that if I could help with even just the meeting notes or remembering where we left off in conversations, I could take some of the mental load off their shoulders. It's a balance to be present and helpful in a stressful situation, and you need the ability to read the room. I never made jokes or disrupted people from talking. My goals were just to show up and show a consistent level of support for them wherever and however it was needed.

I would pay attention and listen to my teammates. If I noticed someone was struggling or overwhelmed, I stepped in and asked the same questions I recommended earlier, "How are you? Are you ok? Is there anything you need clarity on?" These personal but deep questions were appreciated by my team and helped them to feel supported. Once again, this kind of support requires reading the room and knowing when to ask these types of questions, whether that's privately or around others. Tread lightly and always be respectful. Quickly and furiously, we were able to make the necessary privacy adjustments to *Rocket League* to keep the game safe for all players. When we were finished, leadership gave the engineers extra time off to recover from the unfortunate crunch.

When people feel valued and supported, they bring their best and honest efforts, even in the toughest crunch situations. An effective producer understands the person behind the work and helps them when times are tough. To create an environment where both the team and the game can thrive, accountability must be balanced with compassion. There is no shortcut to making that happen.

A culture of accountability and compassion isn't optional. It is the foundation of successful leadership in game development. Accountability ensures that everyone takes responsibility for their roles, while compassion fosters understanding and trust. These two principles do not conflict. They work together to create a space where teams can thrive under clear expectations while feeling supported through challenges.

Accountability, *an obligation or willingness to accept responsibility or to account for one's actions*, is essential for effective leadership.

You set the tone as a leader by showing that commitments matter and responsibilities are not optional. Holding yourself to the same standards as your team builds trust and proves that rules apply to everyone. This kind of fairness eliminates favoritism and keeps expectations clear.

Accountability is not about punishment or figuring out who's right and wrong. When used properly, it strengthens trust and encourages improvement. When mistakes happen, focus on the cause rather than assigning blame. Using setbacks as learning moments allows the team to refine processes and grow. When people feel supported instead of criticized, they stay motivated, even when challenges arise.

Compassion, taken from its Latin roots, literally means *to suffer with.*

A compassionate team leader recognizes that people are not machines; they have real lives and emotional states. Their circumstances can change, and personal struggles sometimes affect performance. When accountability is handled without compassion, it becomes emotionless and anti-human, draining morale and causing disengagement.

So, what does compassion look like?

Rather than assigning blame, a compassionate leader first asks, "Are you ok? How can I help?" and looks for solutions. That might mean adjusting deadlines when someone is struggling or offering guidance when a team member feels lost. Holding people accountable while recognizing their well-being creates an environment in which both performance and trust can thrive.

When accountability and compassion work together, teams can perform well under pressure and continue producing high-quality work. A group that understands expectations while receiving support stays engaged and adapts to challenges more effectively. This isn't just theory. It's a core part of leadership in game development. This is how we build trust.

I had a junior producer working for me named Danielle. She was career-driven and wanted a promotion to earn more money. Who doesn't want more money in the games industry? We set clear expectations, almost like a checklist for her promotion. Danielle took this list and tried to finish it as quickly as possible to show she was ready for more responsibility. One requirement I set was to successfully run her team's upcoming features and ensure the project and task life cycles were working for her team.

She misunderstood efficiency as just "getting things done faster." Danielle started crunching every night to finish projects on time. I didn't notice until I saw late-night messages from her to the team asking them to do more work. Luckily, this hadn't caused any real problems yet.

When I stepped in, it was tough to explain that efficiency doesn't mean crunching or rushing work. It means working smoothly with the team, using methods like *nemawashi* or *guanxi* to build alignment or solve problems, not taking everything on yourself. Compassion was important here, especially because the accountability fell on me. I thought I'd set clear expectations, but I hadn't. I took responsibility because I felt I'd caused this, and I asked Danielle if we could realign on how to move forward. With open communication and renewed trust, we were able to move forward toward her goal while supporting our team's morale.

Junior producers often fall into this trap. That's why mentors are important. They help guide them through these moments. Producers should look out for everyone on the team, including their fellow producers. *If you want to build great games, focus on creating strong teams.* Leading with accountability and compassion builds trust and drives success. A team's achievements reflect its leader, and prioritizing well-being is one of the best investments you can make in a project's future.

Everything in life is about moderation. We can't constantly push ourselves too hard and only care about results. If we stay up all night playing video games, we will suffer negative consequences the following day. If we stay up all night studying for an exam, we will probably have a headache and reduced brain function during the exam. We can't stay effective at our jobs if we are always doing overtime. We don't measure success only by results and outputs; we measure success by how we achieved those results and outputs. I am not preaching this to you from some place of perfection; I'm guilty of every single one of these examples. In fact, this leads me to one of the more embarrassing personal stories in this book when I had to learn this lesson of moderation myself. I once got so caught up in a competitive, ranked mindset that I pushed myself too hard. This had negative consequences on me personally, but it also affected the team morale of the people around me. Let's get into it.

RANKED VERSUS CASUAL GAMING

Back in 2017, I was completely hooked on *PlayerUnknown's Battlegrounds* (*PUBG*), a battle-royale game created by Brendan Greene and developed at Bluehole Studio. Before we get into the story, though, let's take a brief look at the history of our modern genre of battle royale games. Their roots trace back to *Arma 2*, a military simulator (Mil-Sim) that led to the creation of *DayZ*, a survival mod set in a zombie apocalypse. A **mod** *is a change or alteration to a game made by players or fans, rather than by the original developers.*

As *DayZ* grew in popularity, modders began experimenting with new ideas, including Brendan Greene's own mod *Battle Royale*, inspired by the Japanese film of the same name. His work eventually led him to *H1Z1: King of the Kill*, where he collaborated with engineers at Daybreak Game Company.

Greene always wanted to build his own game. That opportunity finally arrived when Bluehole invited him to develop *PUBG* as a standalone game. *PUBG* was a culmination of the genre up to that point, and I really think it solidified the battle royale before *Fortnite* entered the space.

This brings us back to my story. *PUBG* had a classical leaderboard system that the competitive players used to climb the ladder for the highest ranks. At first, I played casually, dropping into matches with friends while we tried our best to mix stealth and aggression and survive to the end. Unexpected moments of perfect gameplay and the occasional "Winner Winner Chicken Dinner" pop-up for being the last one to survive made every game heart-poundingly exciting.

Growing up, I played many outdoor sports like baseball and football, but I was never a star athlete. When I played football, I was jealous of the running backs and wide receivers who would score game-winning touchdowns and were the heroes of the game. I was always on the sidelines, not good enough to start on the field but good enough to make sure the starting players had enough water to drink. I just didn't have the size or speed to compete with the other kids.

That being said, as you might have picked up on by now, I'm pretty good at video games. I've been playing shooting games for over 30 years, and I am proud of it. If you need me to move a mouse and click on an opponent's head to land that perfect elimination, I'm your guy. *PUBG* made me feel like a star player, and I went all in.

After an astonishing run of ten consecutive wins, I checked the leaderboard. I felt pretty good and was curious about how I ranked compared to other players. To my slight surprise, I had broken into the top 1,000 overall and ranked among the top 100 for kills. That moment lit a fire in me. Was I really this good? If I kept pushing, how far could I go? Could I be the hero of this game and win all the fame and glory the ranked mode had to offer? I saw my future clearly. This was how I could redeem myself after high school and finally soak in the victory and glory of winning.

The problem was that I spent my time with two different gaming groups. One group played casually for fun, while the second group was serious about competition and had to win. To reach my goal of a bright future, I had to make a tough choice between the two groups. I had to choose who to play with based on who could help me achieve my goals in the game.

I wanted to see how far I could go. I decided to tell my casual gaming group that I couldn't play with them as much because I wanted to win, and frankly, they weren't good enough. My competitive friends and I formed a squad. We became a force that reminded me of my best days in *Counter-Strike*. The adrenaline rush was intoxicating. Victory after victory propelled me higher on the global leaderboards.

But as the grind intensified, something began to gnaw at me. My "casual friends" were still friends and would invite me to play with them, but I always hesitated to join. I would probably lose playing with them, which would tank my ranking, and I couldn't risk it. They noticed, of course. "Why are you so serious about this?" one asked, his tone a mix of confusion and disappointment. "It's just a game."

They weren't wrong. When we lost, my competitive friends and I would get into shouting matches about whose fault it was. Sometimes, it wasn't just a game to us. However, at the time, the perspective of my casual group clashed with my obsession for winning and climbing the ranks. *What's the point of ranked gaming if you're not trying to be the best?* I wondered.

But then the opposite question lingered just as strongly: *What's the point of playing the game if you're not having fun, and it's all serious all the time?* As I continued to play, I had pushed my way into the Top 50, then finally cracked the Top 10 on the leaderboards. One late night, after an intense, hard-fought victory, I instinctively went straight to the leaderboards to see where that win had taken me. There it was. I had climbed to #2 globally, just one step away from being the highest rank in the world. This was it. I was about to be the best, and everyone would know it.

As I stared at the screen, though, that rush of triumph was suddenly replaced by an unsettling thought.

> *What happens if I actually make it to #1? Then what?*
>
> *Would I keep grinding to maintain it?*
>
> *Or would I step away with the satisfaction of having "been there, done that"?*

Let's pause my story for a moment here and really look at this thought process.

The game had been getting so stressful that it was no longer fun, so I was questioning myself. Why was I going so hard?

Looking back, I realized I've had this same experience working at a couple of game studios, where it felt like we were so serious that we forgot to have fun.

Why does this happen, though?

Some people believe playing ranked games is about competing at the highest level to prove your worth. We are human creatures, and I believe this drive for greatness and recognition appears in most of the things that we try to do. I see some people take on this mindset of great ambition when they join the games industry. They are already aspiring to join top-tier studios to make their mark, and they have the will to work as hard as possible in order to achieve that.

While I understand this mindset, it's important to recognize that this is not the only path to success.

Gamers have consistently shown that, whether you're a ranked player or a casual one, you can still achieve your goals. There are multiple game modes, and not every game mode needs to be ranked.

Take streamers and influencers on platforms like Twitch and YouTube. Many, or probably most, aren't known for their high-level skill or leaderboard positions. Instead, they thrive on playing games, being entertaining, and leveraging humor, personality, and charisma to captivate their audiences. Many people play video games that do the same thing, who are not streamers or influencers. You are probably one of them.

There are many video game producers in the industry that fall somewhere between the ranked and casual of game development.

On one side, there are those who approach development with a singular drive to create the best game ever, pouring every ounce of their energy into their craft. On the other side, some teams prioritize camaraderie and enjoyment, viewing game development as a job to be enjoyed rather than a mission to revolutionize the industry. Both approaches bring value, but as professionals, we need to learn to strike a balance between these extremes.

The sweet spot lies in blending the best of both worlds. The goal isn't to chase perfection at all costs, nor get lost in the relaxed atmosphere of casual fun. It's about embracing a professional developer mindset. Professional developers understand that games are both art and business. They keep a sense of fun while staying focused on the practicalities of delivering a successful product. They push for excellence without forgetting the human side of development.

Going back to the *PUBG* story, in the middle of all this mental conflict, I decided to look up who was in the #1 spot on the leaderboards. This was the person I would have to beat.

I'm not sure what I wanted to find out, but what I did discover about him made my decision for me. I wanted to find out whether he had uploaded any YouTube videos or was a streamer. Searching on Twitch.TV, I discovered he was a small streamer who occasionally uploaded videos of his matches. Watching his playing style was eye-opening and the final nail in the coffin for me on this journey.

This player did whatever it took to win his games, which meant prioritizing survival over fighting. He did this by moving cautiously, staying on the edges of the circle, and only engaging when he had no other choice. It wasn't a bad strategy, far from it. It was effective. But it was the complete opposite of how I played. I wanted to go in guns blazing.

I had built my climb on aggression, taking every opportunity to find and win fights. Watching his videos, I realized that my approach, one that so many might consider reckless, had propelled me all the way to #2 on the global leaderboard.

And the truth?

I didn't want to play against someone who was just going to hide in a house, forcing me to check every single corner, a style we call "camping." I realized that my #2 rank was enough for me. I didn't want the title of #1 because I knew in my heart that my playing style required more skill, and I was proud of what I had accomplished.

If I'd looked up his strategy earlier, maybe I wouldn't have even tried to climb so high; it was that different from what I enjoyed about the game.

But now, knowing what I knew, I realized I didn't need to counter his playstyle to take the top spot. He could keep it. I was content with knowing that I had made it as far as I had by playing the game on my own terms.

This put an end to one part of my mental battle, but I was still spinning thoughts in my head and needed to question my intentions again. Should I be casual or play ranked video games? I still loved the thrill of climbing, but was I having fun? Was I the person I wanted to be while grinding for rank?

I reached out to my casual friends, the ones I'd left behind in my pursuit of rank. "You guys up for a game?" I messaged, half-expecting a snarky reply.

Instead, they welcomed me back as if no time had passed.

Looking back, chasing the #1 spot wasn't just about the leaderboard; it was also about discovering what kind of player I wanted to be. Along the way, I had proved to myself that I could compete at the highest levels. But more importantly, I had learned what really mattered to me in gaming.

For some players, it's about the title, the recognition, and the rank. And that's okay. But for me, it was about the journey, the thrill of the fight, the bonds formed with friends, and the memories made along the way. Whether it's ranked play or casual lobbies, the key is finding joy in the experience, not just the destination.

So, I never did become the #1 player in *PUBG*. And that's fine by me. When I think about my time in the game, I don't see a number on a leaderboard; I see a collection of stories, victories, and friendships that made every match worth it. And that, to me, is winning.

And this is the mindset I want to have both as a gamer and as a video game producer. When I show up to work, I want it to be about making a great game. But I also want my day to be filled with interacting with coworkers, solving problems, and creating an environment where world-class artists and designers can do their best work. And that's what every chapter in this book is about: capturing the methods and techniques that producers can employ to make every day at work both effective and enjoyable.

Ok. You have actually reached the end of Part Two now. I hope these thoughts and stories have helped you to create a strong foundation as a video game producer and offered alternative viewpoints to current industry standards. To help reinforce these concepts and keep them fresh, I have created Part Three of this book, "The Training." This final section is a guide to honing your skills as a video game producer across all your favorite types of video games, from the past, today, and the future.

PART THREE - THE TRAINING

If you were to ask me, "Hey Casey, how can I improve at video games?" I would say, "You should play more video games!"

If you asked me, "How can I improve at my job?" I would say, "You should play more video games!"

If you asked me, "How can I improve my relationships?" I would say, "You should play more video games!" (On the other hand, if your relationships keep failing, maybe you are playing too many video games.)

The essence of this book is that the skills you learn in video games can be applied to the real world, whether that's in your schooling, career, or personal relationships. Video games give us a place to practice and train several skillsets with others or by ourselves. I want to explain how we can use all the leadership and manager concepts we just discussed in the two previous sections of the book, and find practical approaches to applying them in any of your favorite digital worlds.

The point I want to drive home is that working with others in video games is a very unique skill with great benefits for your career and personal life. No formal class will teach you the actual ability to lead and communicate like video games will. Of course, there are other avenues to learn similar skillsets; two that come to mind are *Toastmasters* and Improv Classes.

Toastmasters is a worldwide nonprofit educational organization with clubs in more than 140 countries. These clubs get together to practice public speaking and leadership skills in a supportive group setting. This international social club follows a structured format that gives people the opportunity to give speeches in front of groups of others. The listeners provide feedback and ask questions, which helps the presenter gain confidence in presenting in front of others and practice responding in the moment. They have other roles for members who help mentor or organize the events throughout the year.

The second approach I've often heard recommended by successful businessmen and Hollywood actors is theater improv classes. These are a great way to practice active communication and confident leadership. Improv, or impro, is short-hand for improvisation. This is a type of spontaneous theater practice with no script that requires participants to play off one another to create an engaging scene. The ability to react and keep a conversation going is a powerful skill many people value. In my opinion, improv and social speaking clubs have immense value, but I feel like the limitations are far too many.

The greatest value those clubs bring is the personal interactions with others, but unfortunately, that can cause the first barrier.

Theater companies are physical businesses with brick-and-mortar buildings that are only open at certain times during the week for certain durations. It requires people to leave after work or on weekends to meet up with others at these locations, which can be a big commitment depending on the distance.

Whether it's a class or a social club, both usually require a financial commitment through monthly fees or membership requirements. Financial burdens are real, and some can't justify recurring payments for this type of practice. Depending on where you live, you can always check your local community to see if there are free community-based classes available as well.

Regardless, the most prominent barrier I see is the literal leap to practice communication and leadership with other people in person. Not everyone is extraverted enough to cross that bridge, which was very true for me as well. There is something more comfortable about the anonymity you have in video games. It's easier to make a mistake in that anonymity versus making a mistake in a real-life setting with a person 2-3 feet away from you. To ask an inverted person to go to work or school, then afterward drive to a class, pay for it, spend physical energy and mental energy interacting with others in person, only to drive back home and likely need to go straight to bed, is asking a lot.

Now, my option to pursue video games as a training mechanism also has barriers.

First, there is the fundamental need for an electrical source to power the devices you might want to own. Video games need to be played on specific platforms, and you need to purchase equipment such as a personal computer (PC), a console (PS or Xbox), or a handheld device (Switch, iOS, or Android). The most obvious thing is that you need to purchase the game you want to play. We've already seen AAA titles reach price ranges of $100 USD. Even many free-to-play game titles have paywalls (barriers or limited access to the game unless you pay for the content). Fortunately, the range of games and their price points is broad enough that many of the different skills and techniques in this book can still be applied.

If we are talking about an online game that requires an internet connection, we also need to consider internet costs and charges. Even if you can afford it, the quality and output strength of your internet can be an issue. I've been excited to see how much progress is already being made globally to get more people connected online. This is a barrier that might be greatly reduced for others very soon in the future.

With all of these items put together, gaming enables you to focus on and practice the skills you want to improve on from the comfort of your own home, with fewer time restrictions. The limitation of finding other people to practice with is greatly reduced. Not all of your favorite games will have people in their servers populated enough to practice these skills, but the different types of games out there are vast and have players actively in them. There are over three billion gamers in the world, so there is always going to be a game populated somewhere for you to find.

Not all games need an internet connection, and single-player games are just as valuable. I hope I have clearly shown enough examples from certain RPGs or tactical games that help you flex your game-intuitive mind. Playing against NPCs with certain restrictions or morale goals can be very diverse in its ability to practice and learn a certain skill.

This third part of the book dives deeper into how video games, both with and without restrictions, can be practiced to learn the skills in this book. To future-proof this section as games go out of date and shut down, I will organize it by genre, using stereotypical playstyles rather than relying on titles alone.

Games will come and go, but the fundamentals of genres will always be well defined. A first-person shooter will always be a shooting game with the player's camera in the first-person position. An MMORPG will always be a role-playing game in a server-based setting that can host a large number of players online.

As video games continue to age, change, and evolve, it will become easier (and more complex) to categorize them. Here is a brief breakdown for genre reference, along with a list of the modern (as I write this) game titles in that genre.

Genres	Example Games
Multiplayer Online Battle Arena (MOBA)	*League of Legends* *Defense of the Ancients*
First Person Shooter (FPS)	*Counter-Strike* *Valorant* *Overwatch* *Call of Duty*
Real Time Strategy (RTS)	*Starcraft* *Warcraft* *Command and Conquer*
MMORPG	*EverQuest* *World of Warcraft* *Final Fantasy Online* *Ashes of Creation*
RPG / Strategy	*Baldur's Gate* *Civilization Series* *Skyrim Series*
Large-Scale Coordination FPS	*ARMA* *Battlefield Series* *Squad* *Hell Let Loose*

Resource Management	*Stardew Valley* *Minecraft* *Farm Simulator* *Factorio*
Roguelike/Roguelite	*Dead Cells* *Hades* *Windblown*
Battle-Royale	*Fortnite* *H1Z1* *PUBG*
Co-Op Survival / Extraction Shooters	*Tarkov* *Arc Raiders* *Ark Survival*
Sports	*FIFA* *Madden NFL Series* *Gran Turismo*

As you know, there are way more game genres than what is listed above. If I do reference video games in certain genres, please understand that video games are like music artists. They, too, can easily change genres.

The following training guide is broken out into four significant learning areas. Each area looks at certain skills that can be learned through specific genres. These four areas are:

1. **Leaderships!** *(Producer skills related to leading)*

2. **Systems!** *(Producer skills related to managing human systems)*

3. **Teams!** *(Producer skills related to being on a team)*

4. **Relationships!** *(Producer skills in socializing)*

All of these significant areas do see some overlap in the training abilities being used. For example, communication and leadership can be applied to every section in one way or another. You could argue that the Teams and Relationships sections go hand in hand, but we try to break them out into separate categories to deep-dive into specific lessons. The Teams section focuses more on the structure and coordination within larger teams, while the Relationships section deep dives into the tools and techniques we use to identify, build, and sustain those relationships.

For each genre, I will provide a rating system for how I score the ease of practice within those genres. I believe you can practice most skills in most games, and I encourage everyone to try it themselves. But some genres are naturally easier to practice, while others might be considered harder

The Rating Scale:

The rating is one to five, with one being a harder genre to practice certain skills. Meanwhile, a genre with a score of 5, I think, is the biggest bang for your buck. After the ratings, I will discuss my rationale and analysis of those games and how you can apply or adjust my suggestions. Please be encouraged to challenge my ratings and come up with your own.

This section is set up as a short workbook with Key Objectives to focus on and tasks that I call "Missions" to take on and consider while playing in these genres. You can challenge yourself to complete these missions in the games that you are playing. If you can complete some of these challenges, you are ready for the next step: applying these skills to your classes or careers.

I hope this puts a fun spin on gaming. Enjoy!

LEADERSHIPS!

L eadership is everywhere in games, and it's not limited to just online experiences with others; you can find it in single-player games, too. In games like *Baldur's Gate* or the *Fallout* series, your actions and interactions with other non-playable characters (NPCs) are similar to the real world. You can still practice being a servant leader with your choices, even if it isn't with a real person. See what happens if you try to backstab NPCs in those games, or go against your word, or try to be their best friend without any coercive behavior. Will these computers react and give you the same results?

Online games with team gameplay still offer the advantage of experiencing leadership with others. If there is any direction at all happening in any game that you play, someone is leading, and that means others are following. This is an opportunity to practice or observe some of the most important skills for being a producer, which are the soft skills that we now call "Leading."

Leading emphasizes *goal setting and creating culture by driving change*. It involves guiding the team by setting a cultural example that fosters collaboration and motivates individuals to contribute their best work toward the goals.

As discussed in the first part of the book, leading encompasses many techniques and methodologies that shouldn't be overlooked. If we want to bring players together to accomplish a goal, then we must consider servant leadership and its principles. When we apply those principles in the games we play, you will notice how much easier it is to transform another gamer's goal into a shared vision with you.

When you want to practice being a better leader in games, remember the power of foresight. Leaders are driven to look forward and prevent disasters or wrong turns later down the road. The focus and consistency in protecting the shared goal and the team's well-being are what leaders earn respect for. With that respect gained, you can use different types of powers: coercive, manipulation, or persuasive powers to understand their strengths and weaknesses.

If you are leading in games, analyze your experiences to grow and learn from them. You can start by asking yourself: Why are people following you? How often do people not listen? If you can remember a specific example, ask yourself what made it work or not. Was it the style of the communication or the situation at hand?

In video games, you don't need to lead at first, and sometimes it's easier to start by following. Followers listening to leaders can also observe what works and what doesn't for them. If you are following another leader in the game, take note of what they are doing. Why are people following them? Does this game have common goals that everyone follows, or is the in-game leader actually providing direction?

Do their goals and directions make sense? When you listen to them give directions, is it clear what they mean? How many other people are following, and how many other people are confused?

How often is the leader you are following right? If they are using foresight and helping identify a problem, did it actually help prevent it? How often are they false alarms or the boy who cried wolf with wrong foresight? When it did prevent a big disaster, what techniques or abilities was the leader using? Were they using wisdom or intuition?

Let's dive into how these lesson focus areas can be taught in the genres below.

- Lesson Focus Areas:

- Servant Leadership and Shared Visions

- Types of Power and Influence

- Foresight and Adaptability

Best Genres to Practice in:

Tactical Shooters	
Co-Op Survival Games	
MOBAs	
MMOs	
Strategy Games	

Why These Genres Are a Great Place to Practice Leadership:

1. Matchmaking, Simple Objectives, Built-in Comms

When looking at this lesson's focus areas, repetition will be the key to mastery. I focused on genres that have stereotypical playstyles or features that make it easy to practice games in. For me, that would be games with "matchmaking" abilities, an automatic way to group players into a server to play a game. Second, games with easy-to-understand goals and objectives, like "destroy the enemy team." Lastly, I looked at genres that tend to have built-in voice communication so that players don't have to do any setup of their own.

Quick matchmaking allows players to repeatedly practice leadership and teamwork skills in a short time. Most games highlight this accessibility by prominently displaying a "Play Now!" button on their title screens, instantly connecting players to matches. This makes these game types highly approachable and effective for repetitive skill development, which is why they are the highest-rated.

Tactical shooters, co-op survival games, and even MOBA-style games typically feature matchmaking systems that quickly pair players for matches. Players typically wait a short 30-second to 3-minute window to join games that last around 10 to 30 minutes. This quick and repetitive cycle requires a low personal time commitment.

If we want to play these games to practice Leadership, we need to start with the shared vision of the players on your team. That first hurdle is greatly simplified if you are playing a shooter or even an MOBA, as the goals are very straightforward for all players. In an FPS like Counter-Strike or Valorant, the goals are to defeat your opponents and not have them defeat you. This makes it easier for leaders in those games because you don't have to explain anything; everyone already understands. In this case, your leadership strategy is to influence the team toward certain objectives and to call out the tactics you could use to accomplish them.

Here is a direct example. Let's say you are playing a five-player versus five-player shooting game on a map with two different objective sites, A and B. If your team attacks the 'A' site three times in a row and they fail each time, propose a new objective to your teammates: "Let's try to attack site 'B' instead." If you notice the other team has been successfully sniping you from long distances, you can also propose a tactic: "Let's also throw smoke grenades for extra cover from the snipers in the back." If you influence your team with this method of leadership, you have a greater chance of accomplishing the goal of winning the game.

Structure of leading in-game

If you are not interested in shooters, try looking for a game that has good built-in communication tools, even if they are not centered around voice chat. There are so many clever ways to communicate, and games like *Rocket League* have incredible quick chat systems that can convey tactics with a click or two and a few words on screen. Other games might have ping systems or public maps with information updated in real time. Most of the games in these genres do have built-in voice communication, though, and if it is safe to do so, I would recommend using it. If we are trying to practice for the real world, it is so much stronger to practice with your own voice in these games.

The ability for gamers to use voice comms (communication) is the best way to communicate in video games. Our voices are powerful tools, and can convey so much through tone and cadence as well as through words. Video game lobbies are the best learning grounds for this experience. Leading is not about barking out objectives and commands and expecting people to follow; it's also about listening and following others. As you listen, take note of what works with other people and why. Was it just common sense and everyone agreed, or was it the confidence and tone in their voice? Or was it neither, and it merely worked because someone was calling out a direction, and everyone else followed? Take note of any time that name-calling or toxic behavior occurs, and how well those situations turn out. What is the lesson to be learned?

Even in an anonymous voice chat, you need to be able to read the room, so to speak, and pick up on what resonates with the other gamers on your team. This is great practice for what you should be doing in the real world. One thing you will likely notice if you practice reading the room is that instructions, or proposed plans, need to be simple to understand. Complexity and vagueness are usually the culprits when people misunderstand the plan.

Co-Op Survivor and Extraction Shooters offer slightly different trade-offs for practicing Leadership. Most games in these genres have built-in voice tools, as well as all the benefits of matchmaking with fast queue times. In Co-op Survival or Extraction Shooters, however, the objectives can get a little murky. It's not as simple as defeating the enemy since the enemy is not clearly defined. Other players in the game are not enemies automatically, so players have the agency to determine how they want to handle certain situations. You can decide to work collaboratively with other players or be aggressive and take their loot. Players are usually an obstacle while the main objective is extraction with loot or gear. These dynamics can cause the goals and objectives in the game to vary.

This nuance gives Co-Op Survivor games a unique perspective on communication. Often, the players on voice chat have open communication with any other players nearby, even if you are not on a pre-defined team. This feature is called proximity chat. Because of it, you can talk to nearby players and try to negotiate your way out of potential harm. In this scenario, you can choose to employ one of the three types of power: coercive, manipulative, or persuasive. All three types of power come with benefits and downsides and will lead to different outcomes. This is the best genre of game to actually practice coercive or manipulative power types, as they are an expected and common form of communication in this style of game. And there are enough safeguards in place so that if the situation gets toxic, you can just turn off the proximity chat feature.

But, with proximity chat on, we can try to have fun and role-play a little bit with other players, kind of like being in an improv class. Each encounter would be spontaneous and provide a unique situation for both players. If we look at a game like *Arc Raiders* imagine applying different types of power to see the results in this scenario:

Player 1: "Hey, I hear you moving in that house! Stop and give me all your items, or I'm going to throw grenades in!"

Manipulative Response

Player 2: "Hey, WE heard you moving outside and WE have OUR guns aimed at you. You give us all your items, or it might not look good for anybody."

Coercive Response

Player 2: "You are going to die if you don't leave right now. I'm the best player in this lobby and will ruin your day."

Persuasive Response

Player 2: "Instead of me throwing all my items out, how about I team up with you and help you escape with your gear so that you have a higher chance of survival?"

If you were Player 2, which response would you try? If you were Player 1, how would you react to each of these responses?

This scenario can play out in several different ways. Players can negotiate with force and tell the other players to leave before they attack them. Players can use manipulation to try to trick players into thinking there might be more of them, and if they attack, they will surely die. Or, players can try to use reason and persuasion to convince the other player that they mean no harm. But no matter which option you choose, the fun part of these spontaneous encounters is that we don't know our opponents' true intentions, how they will react, or how the situation will resolve.

This is the perfect place to practice reading the room. In any scenario that requires voice communication, listening is just as important as speaking. You should try to pick up on the intent of other players by their tone or cadence. Just because someone yells doesn't mean their intent is bad, but it doesn't automatically make me assume their intent is good either. The way we smoothly and calmly talk and react could make all the difference, and being able to listen is the key to understanding what tactic will get us closer to our goal.

Remember when we talked about foresight? Foresight is the ability to prevent disaster and find the right path forward by using both our intuition and our wisdom. When you are practicing leadership and working toward a shared goal with others, you can (and should) also use foresight to help find the right path forward. These game types, with the human element added to them, have a wide variety of experiences that can happen and occur, wherein there is never truly a right path forward. They provide you with the opportunity to fail, and when you get it wrong, since it's a short-term and low-risk scenario, you can march right back up and try again.

The best realization you will have as a leader in these fast-paced environments is that it's ok to get it wrong. Someone on either team is getting it wrong every game. Not everyone can be a winner. When you don't win, you can look back at what happened, identify what went wrong, and then queue back up and try to prevent a repeat disaster. It turns out, video games really are a perfect training ground for leadership skills.

2. MMOs and Persistent Worlds

Mass Multiplayer Online Games are actually among the best game genres for practicing leadership and communication. Many of the leadership stories I've shared here were inspired by raid leaders across multiple games. However, MMORPGs also present a significant barrier to entry. Joining an established raid guild typically requires meeting specific criteria, and while starting your own guild isn't particularly difficult, it, among most things in this genre, demands considerable time and commitment.

But let's take a look at what MMOs have to offer. For one, there are usually thousands of players online to play with. Most MMOs give you the ability to group up with and level up with other players. This is good social practice for gamers, but it also has a flip side. Raiding content usually has barriers to entry requiring certain level minimums or specific gear.

Additionally, many MMORPGs lack integrated voice chat,

requiring external tools like Discord or TeamSpeak for effective communication. While these tools are widely used by gamers and generally aren't inconvenient, their use is usually limited to your immediate community, restricting spontaneous interactions with the broader gaming population. Text chats in these games are a more common option available to the players.

The beauty of modern MMOs is that game developers have made the quality of life drastically easier than it was in the early days. You actually have party or group finders, and if you want to raid, there are usually matchmaking queues to get you into a raid group that needs more players. These types of features were needed as games grew more complicated and diversified their levels and skill trees, like crafting versus adventuring, which splits up the player base and requires more advanced team-finding tools.

Some players wanted to craft, others wanted to PvP, and the main cohorts usually raid. As a gamer trying to practice leadership, there are many opportunities here, but they come with a wider range of goals and an additional barrier of the time commitment it takes to reach effective levels. This, too, has a flip side, though. As is often the case with a barrier that requires effort to cross, when you do get to the other side, there is usually a strong and wonderful community to welcome you with open arms. They've fought through the same barriers, learned similar lessons, and are more likely to have a shared goal. Once you are a part of one such group, you can practice servant leadership and help join their shared vision regardless of their niche focus.

If we look at the small-group dynamics in MMOs, they share many of the same benefits as the Shooting and MOBA genres: they are easy to align around goals. In MMOs, small groups are usually queued up into a dungeon together, where the objective is to reach the end and defeat the final boss for its loot. Aligning a group of people around clear objectives and tactics is going to be the key to successful leadership practice.

Imagine a scenario where you are clearing out a dungeon with a group of other players. Halfway through, there is a very tight corridor with more monsters than your team can handle. If you attempt to attack them head-on, you will surely die, as there are too many of them, and there is no way to run by without them noticing you.

This is an opportunity for the group to discuss tactics, and good leaders are the ones facilitating those conversations. Anyone practicing leadership has the opportunity to see conflict resolution and shared agreement in action in this situation. If you could get a group of gamers to align on a single strategy for a dungeon, what leadership skills do you think you would need to make that happen?

The biggest benefit that MMOs provide is the ability to practice foresight, as most decisions in these genres of games require long-term thinking. Unlike quick matchmaking games in non-persistent worlds, the decisions in MMOs have long-term consequences and usually impact other players as well. With crafting and markets being a large part of item acquisition in the game, prices and availability will change based on the current content of the world. These factors cause increases or decreases in the supply and demand. If some major raid content just launched, the prices of health potions and their availability will change as everyone wants to stock up on them.

You have the opportunity in MMOs to practice foresight and adjust your strategies accordingly. If you see a game developer's patch notes for the game saying they are going to release some new content on an upcoming date, you can prepare and stock up on the health potion ingredients prior to that date. Once the content launches to all players, you will be in a better position to sell the materials at a higher price point.

3. Single Player, Strategy, and NPCs

Strategy games like the *Civilization* series or *City Builders* put you in a leadership position running a nation or city. Both involve deep, complex relationships with NPC counterparts, enabling interactions that teach valuable leadership skills and inform decision-making. As a leader, your decisions will inevitably make some NPCs happy and others unhappy. This ever-present tension requires you to pay attention and find the right balance of actions.

Goals can vary from game to game. In a city builder, you want to reach a certain population level or build major infrastructure or buildings. In the *Civilization* series, there are different options from world domination to technology advancements or winning through religious control. Whether playing online against real humans or against NPCs, you need to try to align everyone to the same goals to reach a shared vision.

In political simulation games, the easiest way to get the NPCs on your side is to understand what their goals are. It's a two-way street even for computer opponents. Sometimes, they might let you reach your goal for land expansion if you pay them some gold first to get on better terms with them. Sometimes the NPCs want you to behave or play a certain way, and no amount of gold will satisfy them.

In political simulation city-builders, we need to account for other stakeholders. Sometimes our actions align with their personal goals, culture, or policies; sometimes they do not. Each response is often caused by an action you took. This requires you to think through each action in advance, deciding what you are willing to deal with and what you want to avoid. This is where we can really practice the foresight that helps prevent future disasters.

You get to decide what types of power you want to use with NPC opponents to get them to follow your plans. As a leader, you can choose to work with or against NPCs to accomplish whatever goal you've set. You might find yourself keeping your vision looser and more flexible, since you are managing so many more variables. True leaders in online games or against NPCs know the boundaries and limitations of the game and their gameplay before upsetting the other stakeholders.

It's up to you as the player to enjoy and practice in whatever way you prefer. You can choose to lead or follow to see what traits you appreciate in your leaders. Try to mimic these traits and enjoy the journey.

Key Objectives:

Lesson to be learned	Objective while playing in a game
Identify the type of power being used by others.	If anyone gives you an order, direction, or command by an NPC or a real person, what power is being used?
Identify if anyone is acting as a servant leader to the team you are playing with in your games.	Look around to see who is helping as a servant leader for others. Are there valuable things that should be recognized? Take note if anyone else recognizes these traits.
Anticipate a game or another player's next move.	Before a problem or challenge occurs, can you anticipate and set things up beforehand to mitigate the challenge and solve it faster?

Mission Briefing

Leading can be hard at times. Identifying a goal and choosing tactics takes valuable brain space, especially in a fast-paced game. The difficulty really starts to compound when you try to practice leadership with strangers, since they are unknown entities who might respond in unexpected ways. On top of all that, you are trying to be calm, collected, nice, and persuasive. But don't worry. You got this.

Take charge of a game by showing your leadership skills. While you are in an online game setting, convince other players to follow you to a certain goal or objective. The catch is that you must follow the Robert K. Greenleaf Servant Leader principles and only use persuasive powers. Do not use coercive or manipulative powers. How quickly can you get someone to follow, and in what situations do others not follow?

Tips & Tricks

Look at Robert Caldini's methods of influence as leverage and see how many people will follow you. My favorite options were Authority, Liking, and Social Proof. For Authority, you need to perform well in the game or have some achievements unlocked. For Liking, you need to be funny or trustworthy. Try telling a joke or following the objectives properly. Lastly, to practice Social Proof, watch what everyone else is doing, learn the norms of the players you are playing with, and use the same strategies. Read the room.

Define Your Success

Analyze and identify whether you can consistently get people to follow you and win at the game you are playing. If so, start tracking this data to understand how consistent you are. When it doesn't work, try to understand and use foresight to help prevent those issues down the road.

SYSTEMS!

Systems is the all-encompassing word for the processes and operations that we use while managing. Producers are the architects of the systems they build for their teams. This relationship, when done correctly, is what causes the team's output to force multiply. But recall, when we said 'managing,' we aren't talking about controlling people.

Managing is *focusing on creating consistent systems and modeling desired behaviors.*

We create systems when we want to produce consistent results, because who would want to follow something unreliable? Consistency is not always easy, especially when it involves interacting with other players. So how do we create a system within a short-term game lobby when the only thing we can control is our own behavior? Well, we can turn our behavior into a reliable system that is likely to produce consistent results. For starters, we can keep in mind the golden rule, "Treat others as you want to be treated." We want to be good people and not lie, cheat, or steal, so let's model that consistently at all times. While there will always be outliers, this should create a system that produces respect and creates a fun, safe environment for your online team. This kind of system relies on a very human element, which sounds very similar to another concept we've already covered:

Human Systems Building *is the producer's craft of designing and implementing systems that enable teams to succeed consistently and repeatedly.*

When we play video games, we can practice human systems building pretty easily. Video games are a prime tool for teaching others to create systems, whether by following someone's instructions or creating the instructions ourselves.

Similarly to Leadership, video games offer a great training ground for human systems building because the consequences are almost always negligible. There is more forgiveness for failure or trying different methods; in fact, this is highly encouraged in most video game settings. Who hasn't played a city-simulation builder and created their town too close to a water dam, which later has a catastrophic failure and destroys the city? That's an extremely bad consequence of your decision, but your digital city usually forgives you after you restart and stop it from happening again.

This makes video games the best training grounds for simulating and experimenting with different ways to manage systems. Resources come in many forms, from the things you would expect, like wood, stone, and gold, but also from other factors, like food, population, and happiness. Games that make you consider which levers you can pull to achieve different results are excellent at reinforcing the concepts of force-multiplying results or adding disruptions.

In these missions, we want to focus on becoming production taskmasters and learning to break work into simple, easy steps. As gamers, we have all experienced guides or instructions for some of the most complicated puzzle designs or boss encounters. No matter how difficult the quest, someone has always found a way to explain how to do it. If we hone our ability to clearly communicate specific steps and instructions in the games we play, we can easily transfer this talent into our real-world careers or education.

The more you practice this skill, the more you will see how video games and digital environments are the perfect place to try new things. This is a dream for video game producers who want to practice methodologies like Waterfall, Scrum, Agile, and Lean Six Sigma. If you are playing games like *Minecraft* with other players online, you can find endless scenarios in which to practice management and system building.

The second lesson's focus area in systems is estimating how long something will take. This also has crossover with foresight from the Leadership section prior, but we will dive deeper into genres that really let you flex this muscle and get it to a professional level. As producers, we want the ability to understand how long tasks will take and what dependencies they have so that we can build plans or roadmaps for games. In game development, and with most things in life, we need to be able to estimate a timeframe with some confidence. For example, we want to be able to say, "It will take two weeks to finish this project," versus "It will take between two weeks and up to two months to finish this project."

Once your brain gets into the habit of considering estimations and gauging time intervals for tasks, it becomes almost automatic in most things you are doing. Your brain subconsciously becomes a stopwatch with the ability to remember the timing of a task or project. Another analogy is working in a restaurant kitchen, seeing all the different dishes being cooked and prepared. Each chef in those kitchens is a superb estimator. They know exactly how long certain foods take to cook and when to add the next ingredient with the goal of having several different dishes ready to serve at the same time. This is a valuable skill you can hone in gaming.

As the gamer brain starts to evolve and grow, this is where speedrunning and game skill improvement with a Game-Intuitive Mind (GIM) starts to come in.

The Game Intuitive Mentality *is the ability to recognize when something behaves unexpectedly and figure out how to use it advantageously.*

As production taskmasters, we can break out a project's workload into simple steps. If we use estimation, we can create a clear understanding of how long the project will take, and we can further analyze the project using Lean Six Sigma principles to form the Game-Intuitive Mind.

Systems and estimations naturally lead to optimizations because you are able to measure, analyze, and improve. When we think about Lean Six Sigma and even Speedrunning, many games allow us to try to practice each of these steps. As a quick reminder, the DMAIC process for Lean Six Sigma is as follows:

- Define

- Measure

- Analyze

- Improve

- Control

Speedrunning comes in many forms. It doesn't have to be just completing a level at the fastest speed. You can speedrun crafting, character creation, highest scores, and so on. We can use the DMAIC process and attempt to optimize our results regardless. It can be applied to any type of system you want to beat in a fast manner.

Production taskmasters operate within these systems and break out the identified work into manageable sizes with clear directions. We can then provide estimates to set expectations for how long different parts of the process will take. As we put the system to use, we monitor it closely to continue iterating and improving our results. When trying to apply all of these skills, remember to be curious and apply your Game Intuitive Mindset.

Let's take a look at how this lesson's focus areas can be applied across different game genres.

Focus Areas:

- Creating guides and strategies like a Production Taskmaster

- Estimating how long something is going to take

- Speedrunning and game skill improvement with a game-intuitive mind (GIM)

Best Genres to Practice in:

Resource Management	🎮🎮🎮🎮🎮
MMOs	🎮🎮🎮🎮
Simulation	🎮🎮🎮🎮
RTS	🎮🎮🎮
Online Shooters	🎮🎮🎮

Why These Genres Are a Great Place to Practice Systems:

1. Persistent Worlds and Saved Progress

Resource Management games like *Stardew Valley* or *Factorio,* and even some that are a little more adventure-focused like *Minecraft,* are excellent games in which to practice system building. These types of games have low barriers to entry and are easy to launch to get a game going. There is a wide range of simple and complex games in this genre for all ages. The basic concept is that you are progressing through the consumption of materials or resources while balancing other game design constraints like energy outputs or daylight restrictions.

The easiest entry point to being a production taskmaster in these types of games is to read other players' strategy guides or instructions to better understand the system possibilities. The communities for this genre of game are heavily driven by information sharing. Players who play these games can easily join these communities to create guides themselves and learn how to communicate steps and instructions to other players.

Let's look at the giant of a game, *Minecraft*. If you want to find the most efficient way to craft a certain recipe, there is going to be a guide for that online. Players have spent countless hours optimizing and creating crafting processes that make every recipe super efficient with little waste. For example, players have created an automated system to produce iron ingots through a system known as a golem farm. With a deep understanding of the game and using *Game Intuitive Mindsets,* players have manipulated a game feature to their own advantage.

The system of golem farms was likely not intentional by the creators of the game. Rather, players noticed that if they arranged villagers and beds in a certain way, it increased the chance to spawn an iron golem when the villagers panicked upon seeing a zombie. Players then set up walls or fences to funnel the *Iron Golems* to a killing area where there are hoppers that drop these *Iron Ingots* into chests, ready for you to harvest.

This is one example, from one game, where Lean Six Sigma can be practiced over and over again with your friends to optimize these systems further. There is nothing better than creating a system with your friends and enjoying the results. But the skill of building systems has two parts: building the system itself and communicating it to others. Go online, do some YouTube or Google Searches, and find videos or player guides that have already been created by others. There is no reason to reinvent the wheel or to try something brand new. Find the guide that makes the most sense to you and try to understand its structure. What does the overview statement look like? Do they do a good job of preparing you with a list of items or skills you need to have before you can use the guide? Are the steps or list of work in the guide listed out in simple, comprehensible steps to follow? Resource management games are the perfect place to learn how to build and share systems.

As for other genres to learn this skill, MMOs come in second, but they are tied with the genre of Simulation games. In MMOs, to practice these systems, it's pretty easy to join the game and catch up on beginner guides. Most MMOs have leveling guides for starting areas that players can digest pretty easily and start using. It's generally just more of a time commitment than a mental challenge. If that type of gameplay is something you enjoy, I would embrace these genres wholeheartedly.

Not all guides can easily be followed in MMOs, because many quests have level, equipment, or team dependencies. That being said, once you start to be proficient and want to work on more complex systems, MMOs offer a great place to analyze and create systems. As mentioned throughout the book, the ability to coordinate and make systems gets harder at scale and with larger teams, and MMOs offer the opportunity to work within a large raiding party. While this makes system building more difficult, it also replicates the experience of coordinating real-world projects, as you will on video game development teams.

You can approach the process of learning systems in a very systematic way. If you want to start in an easier way, look at resource management games. The guides for these games should start a little more straightforward and self-explanatory. In *Minecraft*, dig down to find resources like diamonds. This guide would be very short and simple to follow. Literally, dig down until you find diamonds.

When you want to take on a more human systems challenge, switch to MMOs. In MMOs, the guide might be how to get a 20-person raid team to take on a raid boss with three different attack phases and patterns. The 20-person raid team will be broken into healers, damage dealers, and tanks, each with their own roles and responsibilities that will need to change and adapt over the course of the three attack phases.

The point of these lessons isn't to give a direct example in these guides but to teach you the ability to identify systems, manage them, improve them, or remove them. Each year, new MMO games or systems might be released, and it's up to us as gamers to understand how those systems help or disrupt individuals.

In the persistent world category, Simulation Games like *Farm Simulator* are also very accessible and easy to enter, but I feel the burden of realism can sometimes be a little too much, which is why they are not tied to a 5-star rating. When you are managing multiple systems like fertilization, gas for equipment, time of the year, and so on, it adds complexity that isn't the easiest to start with. It's not bad to play in, the exact opposite, you should play these types of games once you want more of a challenge. Similar to even *Sims*, these games are easy, but they are slightly harder to test new systems in and to see the results that you want.

In games like *Farm Simulator*, your hands get a little tied because you are limited by the game rules, which might be preventing you from doing whatever you want. This does not apply to all the games in this genre, but I tend to see this pattern of realism a little more rooted in those styles of games.

2. Short-term Commitment Games with Other Players

RTS and Shooting games also require systems and practice to get better at. My days trying to go pro with my *Counter-Strike* teams are a testament to that. The problem here is that, even though it's easy to matchmake and get practice in these genres, finding a team to play consistently with can be a little difficult. Finding other people to commit to and practice with isn't as easy as in other genres. MMOs have those barriers, but there are so many in-game mechanics with crafting, raiding, and other game features that it helps players find guilds that are recruiting. MMOs are also persistent worlds that the same players come back to. Shooting games are not persistent, and in a matchmaking lobby, you do not know who you are going to get paired up with each time.

If you want to try out different hero combinations in the bottom lane of your favorite MOBA, that requires finding another person willing to be a part of that combo. Taking this example further, let's say you found someone willing to participate with you, but would that person have the knowledge and game understanding to test the systems you are imagining? In some MOBA games, like *League of Legends*, you might see over 100+ different champions to pick from. The expectation that the person you partner up with knows all the champions, or even the right ones for your goal, might be hard to meet.

In *Counter-Strike, Valorant,* or even *Call of Duty*, the rounds and games are very fast-paced, so it's a different style of strategy to be followed than the persistent world, resource management games. In these genres, the strategies are shortened to slang for "strats," and there might be a "strat-caller" on the team, a person who is designated to foresee and decide what strategy the team should implement next. Finding people who want to do this isn't always easy, and then, once again, trying new things and possibly losing in the process isn't that attractive to most other gamers.

Being on one of these teams to practice systems is the first story in this book and was my first step toward leadership. I was fortunate to have four other friends who were committed to the same level of gameplay and growth that I was. To find other gamers online with this same mindset is not impossible, but it is an additional barrier to practicing systems in the shooter genre. If you prefer shooting games and faster-paced genres, then it's important to find out where those communities are meeting up. There might be 3rd-party leagues, like FACEIT or ESEA, or Discord servers where players get together.

Do some research and find where these players are so that you can introduce yourself and start gaming at a higher level with them. Once you do, this is where some of those systems can be put in place, such as how to clear a room and what roles and assignments each team member will have. You can test which utilities or weapons to purchase to help smoke out a dangerous hallway or to make sure no one flanks the teams. These are all systems that taskmasters can practice.

3. Estimating and Optimization Systems

Another part of getting better at systems is the ability to make estimations and optimize what is already in place. All the genres mentioned, across all lessons, are playable with the ability to forecast or estimate. The most effective genre to practice estimating skills is probably resource management. It even says it in the title: you are managing resources. In order to do this, you need the ability to estimate your resources to know how much you have and need before you run out. Players intuitively pick up on the skill to anticipate when they can upgrade or progress to the next tier of technologies.

As a player, you should be trying to understand constraints and bottlenecks. In city-building games with streets and traffic systems, it's interesting to see how road design can cause traffic jams. There is no better real-world example than directing traffic in games to understand what might be causing delays and unhappiness in your digital populations.

Shooting and RTS games also have estimating features that you might not have considered. When playing these games against other players, you need to anticipate their movements. By estimating where their general position is and how long it might take them to reach a part of the map, it informs you how quickly you might be able to cut them off. Being able to estimate map sizes and movements is critical for these games.

In MMOs, in order to plan a good raid with 20+ players, you need to set expectations in the timeline of the raid so you know how long it is going to take. By understanding the content, you can inform your players that you might need 2 hours of their time to get halfway through a raid dungeon. Video games will always be a hobby, and people can only commit to things if they know how long something is going to take. Most of us cannot commit to a completely open-ended window with no cap on time.

The ability to get good at estimating takes time and foresight. With wisdom and intuition working together, we start to form patterns and understand more than just how the system functions, but the duration of them. This is where we recommend trying speedruns in games by reading or watching other players' guides on how to perform them. You get to practice with a prepared production taskmaster and gain an understanding of the baseline for what times are possible, so you can estimate how long it will take you to finish. This is the start of understanding Game Intuitive Mindsets (GIM) by seeing how other players picked up on patterns or found ways to manipulate the game to their advantage.

Speedrunning is possible with process improvement and optimization. We are striving to improve our results and the ability to sustain them every time we attempt a new record or personal high score. Finding games with in-game leaderboards or stat trackers makes this so much easier. If you are focused on how fast you can beat a level, find games that tell you the time so you don't have to write it down. If you are aiming for the highest score, find games that already have an engaged community competing with each other. By using Lean Six Sigma and the DMAIC processes in any games we play, we will achieve better results.

It's important for you to really advance in GIM by trying to practice it yourself. Pay attention in these games when you are making systems and see if there are opportunities for you to make those systems perform at their best. You shouldn't always just follow the game's rules or the game's intent. Sometimes it's a great skill to just have fun, pushing the limits and seeing what happens when you play in a way the game never intended. Also, for individuals who want to join Quality Assurance teams and test video games, this skill is indispensable on those teams.

Key Objectives:

Lesson to be learned	Objective while playing in a game
Identify two systems to see which is better.	Compare two in-game systems by making a checklist of their functions to see which system is more efficient.
Apply foresight and estimation to understand how long something will take.	Track the time spent doing something and make a note of any interruptions or inefficiencies that set you back.
Identify skills or techniques from other players who were applying Game Intuitive Minds (GIM).	What are the techniques, skills, or abilities that you have learned yourself or by seeing other players use them? Are they bending the game rules for their advantage without cheating and exploiting others?

Mission Briefing

Create a leveling guide using Lean Six Sigma principles.

To hone your taskmaster skills, challenge yourself to create a leveling guide for one of your favorite games.

Step 1: Choose a video game with a leveling system/mechanic.

Step 2: Break down and define the system and how it works.

What actions expand your experience? Are there specific tasks that yield more efficient progress? Understanding the mechanics is key.

- Write out the different activities that grant experience (questing, fighting enemies, crafting, etc.)

- Are there experience boosts, double XP events, or buffs (like party bonuses) that give the player more experience?

- Identify what slows progress (long travel times to the quest area, resource requirements, or health recovery downtime).

Step 3: Measure & Analyze

Apply Lean Six Sigma principles by measuring the experience yield from different activities. Create a simple table like the example below.

Activity	XP Gained	Time Taken	Efficiency (XP per minute)
Defeating small enemies	50 XP	30 sec	100 XP/min
Completing quests	500 XP	5 min	100 XP/min
Dungeon raids	3000 XP	20 mins	150 XP/min

Step 4: Create a document so others can iterate on the process.

Based on the results of Step 3, create an optimized leveling guide that prioritizes the most effective methods. Your guide should answer the following:

- What should players prioritize to level up fastest?

- What pitfalls should they avoid?

- Are there alternative strategies for different playing styles?

Are you able to write it so you can share it with others, and they can try to improve it? Document it with a YouTube video, a Reddit post, or anywhere else you want on social media. The only way we can iterate is if we share, and sharing involves some form of documentation.

TEAMS!

Working within a team is the whole point of being a producer. You are a force multiplier for your teams, helping them achieve better results. The larger the team you can gain experience working with, the greater the challenges you can overcome. Large teams require coordination and communication at a scale that most people don't get to see in their lifetime. Growing up, depending on where you lived, a school or school district might be the closest experience you had to organizations operating at a large scale.

When thinking of jobs within giant organizations, government, hospitals, the military, and corporations, they all want to see some experience of you being involved in large teams. Video games have the ability to give gamers experience in how their favorite video game team structures are set up, similarly to the industries they might want to join in the future.

In large-scale multiplayer games, players experience real-world teamwork challenges. Gamers need to communicate and coordinate strategies that not every other gamer will want to listen to. By playing so many hours in these types of games, I have already seen my own share of how players interact with each other and how miscommunication happens in real time. So, the more you experience different types of teams in games, the better you will be at understanding them in the real world. Teams come in all sizes in video games, and even the games that don't have fifty-plus players can still be useful in understanding teams at different scales.

The approach to coordinating with newly met players online can look very different depending on the size of the team. Just like at video game studios, the way you work with smaller development teams will look different than the way you communicate with multiple larger teams at the department level. The key is to identify team structures and hierarchies first, and then, secondly, to understand the culture and policies related to them.

Not all games and teams in games are going to have obvious cultures and policies, and sometimes they are even non-existent. It's important to recognize when they are in place for certain games, and to note how players react to them. If they are not well-defined, that's an even better study case so you can watch what players do in the absence of it.

Some games might have team structures set up with centralized or decentralized decision-making. Just like in video game studios, where developers might have more autonomy, or where leadership is more centralized. It's important to understand the differences, and only then will you be able to see them in the game or in the real world.

For teams to really strive and be successful, it's not just about the structure. Remember this quote from before?

"A team becomes more than just a collection of people when a strong sense of mutual commitment creates synergy, thus generating performance greater than the sum of the performance of its individual members." - Author Unknown

Just as in our Leadership training section, 'strong sense of mutual commitment' refers to the shared vision and goals that bind teams together. With teams at a larger scale, we need to understand that there will be far more diverse team members, and it will be a little difficult to herd all the players (or cats, as some project managers say) in the same direction. It is critical to understand and identify any unique roles other games might have. Just like in a game studio, you will have different roles and positions, each with varying levels of experience. As the team grows, the number of stakeholders increases, and the ability to identify them becomes more important.

Stakeholders *are individuals or groups with an interest in the project.*

When playing games with other gamers, it's important to understand everyone's roles and who shares the same level of interest. Just like in our stakeholder

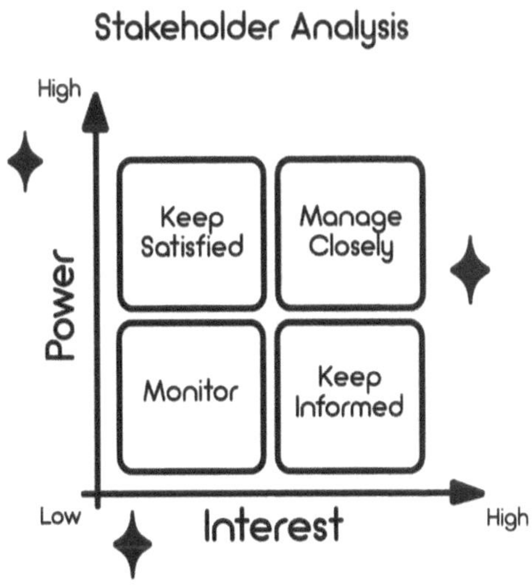

management chart, but it can be expanded a little further when we practice and train. When playing any game, it's important to identify players' interest levels.

If you notice that a player is not on their microphone talking during the match, maybe they aren't interested in playing and are just vibing while listening to music. That probably indicates a low interest. If you notice a player who is talkative and trying to go after objectives, they are someone with a high interest.

The second part of these exercises, when playing games with individuals, is to identify their power level. Sometimes, in community-based servers or persistent worlds, power can be seen if they are a part of the community or just a bystander playing at that particular moment in time. If there are teams, clans, or guilds, those stakeholders might have low or high interests, but their power is likely to be higher. This isn't always an exact formula, and it's good to try to practice on identifying what type of stake the other gamers have in the digital world you are playing in.

We can apply the stakeholder principles to a wide range of roles and players in games. Feel free to come up with your own identifiers for them. In big tactical shooting games, this could look like identifying the medics, assaulters, or snipers. All can be considered stakeholders with different levels of power and interests during the game.

The goal should be understanding and experiencing as many different structures and systems as you can. You want to be able to see what resonates with you, and what you think could be improved. These are the learnings we want to apply to the real world afterward, especially in game development.

After understanding roles and working in different team environments, it will be easier to implement project lifecycle mindsets to take on the next challenge that arises. We don't want to start implementing a project until we understand how the teams are currently working together. It's always supposed to be simple and straightforward:

- We initiate and declare what we want to do.

- We make our plans.

- We start the work as per the plan.

- We check in to make sure we stay on course.

- And when it's over, we pat ourselves on the back and consider it done.

With every challenge you and your fellow teammates encounter, you can take it on with a project mindset. There is a clear goal or shared vision that everyone is working toward. Putting in place a simple project structure to tackle goals is a great way to practice those abilities with others.

The hardest part of this lesson is trying to implement all of this while earning the buy-in and trust of the other gamers you are working with. They will not trust you from the start, as trust is something that is earned. If you are able to produce good results, the other gamers should see the value in what you are trying to do. Once they see value and feel force multiplication working with clarity and confidence, the benefits of results will continue to grow.

Focus Areas:

1. Understanding the structure of teams and shared visions.

2. Recognizing different types of stakeholders to account for.

3. Getting the team to take on a project life cycle mindset.

Best Genres to Practice in:

Large Scale FPS	🎮🎮🎮🎮🎮
MMORPG	🎮🎮🎮🎮🎮
Resource Management	🎮🎮🎮
RTS	🎮🎮
Simulation	🎮🎮

Why These Genres Are a Great Place to Practice Teams:

1. Large Team Structures and Roles to Identify.

I'm a broken record, but if we are trying to practice skills and improve through video games, then we want to get as many repetitions in as we can, and that's why Large Scale Coordination FPS games are rated as a 5 for these lesson sets. The ability to experience large teams in matchmaking, like in the *Battlefield Series*, and be paired quickly with 60+ other players is unique and impressive. There is also a hierarchy or role system in most large-scale shooters, with squad leaders or captains, where there are incentives for players to listen and follow. These games also provide different roles for players to experience and have different play styles to support each other, which are fluid and intuitive.

In this case, it's not just about the repetition, but also about the depth and interactions you can have. MMORPGs are incomparable in this way, hence their 5 rating as well. Yes, there are entry barriers to get into raiding guilds and experience high-level coordination with other serious players, but the experience of working with other players trying to solve problems for a three to five-hour-long raid is impressive. Most Large Team Coordination games are going to be short-session-based, and it's hard to adapt to and practice new coordination with other players in these games, given the lack of the full commitment MMORPGs can provide.

Both MMORPGs and Large Scale Shooters have roles and hierarchy systems that players can be structured into. These give both genres of games great assistance in helping players know who to listen to or what other players are supposed to be doing. In shooting games, if you have a sniper on your team, you automatically understand their playstyle is likely going to be further away from the enemy. An assault class is likely going to be playing up close to the enemy. Understanding their synergies is the best way to practice working together with them, and what type of communication might be useful.

MMORPGs have an entire class structure of healers, damage dealers, and tanks that need to interact in certain ways. Their communication and responsibilities are unique, and many different MMORPGs have different styles. Not all MMORPGs follow the holy trinity structure of roles, and that gives great variety for you to experience. The diversity of roles in all of these genres gives you a unique perspective in working with different types of people.

The key to these skills is to try new roles and immerse yourself in different situations. The best way to understand what another player might be going through is to try playing their role. Being well-rounded in these games helps you understand the limitations or advantages each player might have.

As video games advance, the roles and types of playstyles will advance as well. In the same way, roles at video game development studios will also advance. In the new world of A.I. (Artificial Intelligence), it's hard to say what roles will look like, but the ability to identify and recognize roles and how they function with each other will never go away.

There are major dynamics of team structures that will not change. When you look at flat and tall hierarchy structures with centralized and decentralized decision making in these types of games, you can start to see a pattern emerge. In Large Scale Shooters, structures are usually flat. Decision-making is naturally decentralized because of the fast-paced nature of the shooting games with single goals for the players to accomplish.

This doesn't always apply, but in long-term guilds in MMORPGs, it's more of a tall hierarchy, with administrative roles to fill to support the guild. There are many decentralized decision-making guilds, but you tend to see centralized decision-making from the Guild Owners or their Officer Corps.

The goal should be understanding and experiencing as many different structures and systems as you can. You want to be able to see what resonates with you, and what you think could be improved. Again, all of these observations and learning can be taken to the real world afterward, especially in game development.

You can also take another approach: become a follower instead of a leader on these teams, and start taking notes on what works and doesn't work as a team member. For example, I was playing *Hell Let Loose*, a similar game type to Squad, set in World War II. We were in a game and losing with five minutes left on the scoreboard, no possible way to victory. Our platoon leader left the game, and another player joined our squad and took the platoon leader role. If he could read the room right, he should have realized that the team was taking it casual since it was a hard defeat. He came in barking orders and telling everyone to snap out of it. This was not received well. Other team members yelled at him, and we all got labeled as lazy, and he left the team before saying we were horrible teammates in the global chat channels.

That is not what you should do on a team, and you can learn these lessons by simply watching what makes other teams succeed or fail. Understand the dynamics, use the skills from servant leadership, and find out what the best thing to do is for each situation.

2. NPC Teams and Stakeholders

When we look at the 'Teams!' lesson plan, it feels like the concepts of teams should only be practiced in online games. But the beauty of video games is how many different genres and types of games there are for every type of player. If we look at how the genres Resource Management and RTS play into these lessons, a strong feature they have is the ability to be played offline.

In RTS games, you usually play as the 'commander,' the one directing all of your troops and armies to destroy your opponent. In these types of games, in a single-player setting, it's extremely valuable to understand how you can structure your armies together. What groupings can you put them in? What combination of units synergize together, and which do not?

For example, in medieval combat games where you move legions of armies, there might be a limitation on how far they can march. How many food supplies they have or their morale can affect your choices. Usually, when your armies get to a large size, it takes longer to move them around, or they might take up more resources. We learn that the limitations of bigger teams are that they move slowly.

Sometimes, the political systems in these games add a dynamic that you must consider while preparing the next big move. This is where you can also consider stakeholder management. Who are the other computer opponents you are currently going up against, and what are their dynamics and intentions? If we wanted to categorize these stakeholders into manage closely or keep satisfied, it's very possible.

It's also important to understand the structures and synergies of your opponents, even when just playing against the computer. Understanding which armies or units they might be building will also help determine their weaknesses and the strategies we should execute. This counterbalance of building your armies while ensuring they can counter the opponent is a very agile way of thinking, just as in game development, when problems arise.

In single-player simulation games, like city builders or political medieval games, there are also concepts of allies and trade routes with other cities or nations. Computer stakeholders are just like real people; they usually have an intention or goal in mind that they are trying to accomplish. Understanding their team structures and stakeholders can help you find the right allies in your game. There might be a very fruitful trade route that could give you and your other friendly nations more power if identified properly.

Yet, in all these games, whether online or not, the players you interact with might share a vision that is easy to understand. When working with large teams in these games, it's important to tap into the strategies, visions, pillars, and tactics they use with their teams. This transitions to the Project Lifecycle Mindset.

3. Project Lifecycle Mindset

After understanding roles and working in different team environments, online or offline, it will be easier to implement project lifecycle mindsets to take on the next challenge that arises. We don't want to start implementing a project until we understand how the teams are currently working together. It's always supposed to be simple and straightforward:

- We initiate and declare what we want to do.

- We make our plans.

- We start the work as per the plan.

- We check in to make sure we stay on course.

- And when it's over, we pat ourselves on the back and consider it done.

For any type of game you play, you can use this structure. Its straightforward, common-sense approach is always useful.

If we are playing a game with our friends or strangers online, this is where project mindsets can come into play. We, as gamers, can spin this into a dialogue similar to this:

Player 1: "Hey, everyone, I want us to attack the base on objective B."

- "The plan is to split us up into two groups to pincer attack the main buildings."

- "Let's start the attack in 30 seconds. I will lead the attack on the left, and Player 2 will lead the attack on the right."

- While attacking the left side, "Player 2, how are you doing? Are you progressing toward the objective?"

- After it's done and hopefully completed, "Thanks Player 2, our attack worked and we were in sync with each other."

Project completed.

The important factor in this lesson is to focus on how this applies across any game or project in the real world you want to get done. This system has guardrails to check in and adjust if things aren't going according to the plan.

In some types of RPG games, there are ultimate weapons or quest lines that are complex and take a long time to complete. Using a project lifecycle mindset in this scenario can provide a clear way to coordinate and get the job done.

In these questlines, there are moments where you need to do solo activities, and there are usually moments where you need your friends to come in and support. Creating a project plan that identifies when you need support and when you do not will make everyone's life easier. It's always terrible to be helping friends out in games, and you are just waiting for them to figure out the next step. Imagine having a plan in place to know when you need to show up and what monsters, items, or bosses you need to defeat together.

Since we can apply the project mindset to any genre or game, the biggest value is finding other players who will appreciate it. Even in the *Counter-Strike* stories from early on, and managing my team of friends, I took on this project mindset. I made sure our goals were clear and that everyone was aligned with what we were trying to do. If that was a new map to learn callouts and strategies, or even just to schedule matches with our next opponents. It just breaks it out into easy to understand phases to know where you are even within the project.

A plan and a project mindset with a team can go a long way.

Key Objectives:

Lesson to be learned	Objective while playing in a game
Understanding role specialization.	Understand what each role does in a team for the game that you are playing. How do other classes perform, or how do weapons differ?

Following and executing orders.	Observe how teams organize themselves and put yourself in the middle of it all. Follow someone else's directions and see what works and what doesn't work.
Scaling communication.	Large groups need to communicate differently from smaller groups. What are the common methods teams are using, and how do behaviors differ?

Mission Briefing

Identify a system that players follow in a game that no one has instructed them to follow. There is no rule, design feature, or reason why players should be doing that action. See if you can replicate the results and influence the start of a new system.

How to Execute:

1.   Identify Existing Unofficial Systems:

   •   Do players instinctively line up at a particular spot before a raid?

   •   Are there unwritten rules on who gets the loot in the game?

   •   Do players stack or position themselves in a specific formation in PvP without formal discussions?

2.   Test Influence by Creating a New System:

   •   In a battle royale, start pinging ammo drops for your squad with a double ping each time to start a trend that double pings mean ammo. See if they reciprocate.

   •   Establish a pattern of dropping excess gear near the spawn in a looter game. Do other players catch on and start it on their server?

3. Observe when players start adapting your system:

- Do players begin mimicking your behavior once they start to see the value?

- Does your action become a system that the team follows without discussion?

- Are new players adopting the system just because they see it happening?

RELATIONSHIPS!

Success in production is not just about managing schedules or hitting deadlines. It is also about working with people in harmonious ways. The key to creating a positive and productive team environment is building strong relationships and having effective, transparent communication. Multiplayer games provide a natural space in which to develop these skills and meet other types of communities you might not have experienced before.

Have you ever heard of a successful team where everyone hated each other? How often have you ever heard of companies or sports teams saying they won through fear and anger? There are moments of negativity or fighting, but they are not sustainable for the relationships of a team that wants to stay together. As human beings, we want to be happy and at ease; no one wants to be in a consistent fight with others.

Socializing in games is more than just casual conversation. Sometimes, these groups and communities can be like a second family. It could be VR chat rooms or role-playing guilds where the community and interactions far exceed anything else. These aren't just other gamers anymore; at this point, they are your friends. I have so many friends I have met online, and we have all crossed the globe for each other now to see each other at weddings or vacations. The bonds in games with others are just as valuable as the bonds you might have with people in the physical world.

To sustain these types of relationships with other players takes practice and time. Far more than most casual gamers would want to normally commit to in a way that I think is often overlooked. Anything truly meaningful is worth the effort. I suggest you recall a time when this happened to you and try to understand why. Have you ever made a friend online or through video games? As always, the opposite question is just as valid: have you ever made an enemy or grown to dislike someone else through video games?

Relationship building for producers is just as valuable as technical skills in video game production. Knowing how to form strong connections makes teamwork more efficient and enjoyable. When we talk about relationships, there needs to be a certain level of trust. Every type of relationship you have will have varying degrees of trust as well. Before we can start to form bonds and earn trust, we need to recall these two terms:

Accountability, *an obligation or willingness to accept responsibility or to account for one's actions.*

Compassion, which, from its Latin roots, means *to suffer with.*

These two things should always be a priority, whether you are in the real or digital world. With accountability and compassion, we can show more empathy for each other and build better communities. These skills are also very easy to practice, and I think they become contagious when done right. When you are with other gamers, consistently owning up to mistakes or showing empathy in frustrating moments will create trust. As leaders, these simple, consistent actions in relationship building are how we lead by example.

But the world is not a perfect place, and neither are the digital worlds we might encounter if we try to practice these things. Remember that some players might not want to engage with you, and not all players will behave well. As mentioned before, toxic behavior in video games is still rampant, and unfortunately, we are more likely to have a negative experience online than a positive one.

I honestly do believe that we can change that culture and embrace a positive mindset of competitive challengers trying to compete and win. Yes, you can take games seriously in attempts to get the highest score, and still not have the desire to insult your opponents personally. It is possible to have fun and relax after a day of school or work with video games, building relationships, and not hating on others.

In these focus areas, we have an opportunity to put into place relationship-building techniques that can work. We can understand how to resolve conflicts and have empathy for the other players you are enjoying a game with. As producers, we have a fundamental understanding of Maslow's Hierarchy of Needs when it applies to our teams. We understand that people need to have a stable life to ensure they can perform their best. People have good days and bad days, and it's important to be able to identify situations where you might be able to prevent a negative spiral.

Gamers are no different when we all play together. To play at our best, we need to consider these factors. Our best is not just about peak performance and winning the game; our best also includes our behavior and how we treat the people around us. Video games take up a ton of mental processing power, and having a healthy body and mind is always going to make it easier to excel at them. We must remember to take care of ourselves first if we ever want to consider taking care of others. Eating healthy, sleeping an appropriate amount, and recommending others do the same are always beneficial.

In games, just like in the real world, we need to solve conflicts with each other. Whether you realize it or not, we are consistently doing this with all the other players from the second you first meet in a lobby. We discuss the strategies or plans we want to execute, and we need to reach quick agreements to pull them off. Every time players play games, they do so thousands and thousands of times, which, if you think about it, is an impressive amount of communication and strategy resolution. We can succeed in these microinteractions if we consistently use our persuasive power, not our coercive or manipulative power.

As teams continue to grow in size, it's harder to keep them together and aligned to shared goals. This is usually where relationships start to collapse as the companies or communities grow too large for leaders to maintain. I believe the *nemawashi* technique should be more widely known to combat this decline in relationships. Fortunately for us gamers, there are many games where we can practice the art of *nemawashi* and find more ways to get teams to agree.

Nemawashi describes *laying the groundwork for change by engaging with individuals informally and gathering support before publicly presenting an idea or decision.*

The key thing to remember with *nemawashi* is that it's slow to consensus but fast to execution. It takes social capital to execute, and you also need to focus on relationships to pull this off. It's very difficult to lay the groundwork in video games with other gamers in a 30-minute time span, but it is possible. Sometimes it's easier to get their support on a decision by understanding what type of influence you are using in your communication with them. If we recall our modified version of influence types, we have authority, liking, and social proof to use when engaging with other gamers.

In games, there are multiple ways to have private conversations with other players if direct message or private whisper systems are enabled. On platforms like *Steam*, every player has a Steam profile that is easy to reach out to, and *Steam* has its own chat system where you can engage those individuals informally.

Relationships are core to being on a team, and when you start to participate in a consistent team or community of individuals, you will also grow your *guanxi*.

Guanxi *is a network of personal relationships and the obligations and influence associated with them.*

Once you have found strong *guanxi* with others on your team, it makes many social problems easier to resolve. Gaining alignment through *nemawashi* or other methods requires social capital, which these strong relationships provide. When considering these relationships, the key to these lessons is to find ways to apply them to the real world, such as in your career or at school. Take a look at your relationships with others in-game. Do you notice a pattern that you want to emulate in the real world? Do you notice patterns that you would never use because of your anonymity?

If you are a nice, caring person while playing games with others, and if you take time to find alignment and agreement on problems and decisions with others, and, lastly, if you care about relationships and see the value in them, you are ready to be Maslow's Producer.

Focus Areas:

1. Maslow's Producer

2. Nemawashi

3. Guanxi

Best Genres to Practice in:

MMORPGs	🎮🎮🎮🎮🎮
Large Scale FPS	🎮🎮🎮🎮🎮
Action Adventure	🎮🎮🎮🎮
Simulation	🎮🎮🎮
Resource Management	🎮🎮🎮

Why These Genres Are a Great Place to Practice Relationships:

1. Social and Role-Playing Teams

Relationships can form quickly, but to build real bonds with another person, it takes time. MMORPGs, as a genre, still shine bright as a 5-star rating to build relationships with other players. So far, we've focused on the competitive nature of these games with their intense raiding guilds, but that isn't the only type of guild that players participate in. Social and community-driven guilds are also huge in these games.

My favorite is a Role-Playing Guild where all the players role-play as their in-game character. If you could come up with a backstory, appearance, and personality for your character, you could join this type of guild. It was an incredibly fun experience when everyone shared the same goal and stayed in character while playing together. With everyone committed, the social experiences were fascinating and unique. It is the truest form of self-expression to be whoever you want in a role-playing setting. It's why *Dungeons and Dragons or tabletop* games perform so well as party games with friends. In *Dungeons & Dragons,* you role-play at a table with people physically in front of you, but why can't this be done in our favorite games as well?

The action-adventure genre also includes a great series called *Grand Theft Auto,* which features a vast world with various vehicles and outfits for your characters to wear. Role-playing communities have emerged in this game as well, where some players act as police officers and others play citizens trying to break the law without getting caught. The amount of creativity players can find in these social environments is one of a kind. Instead of improv classes with their many barriers to entry, these games with role-playing environments offer an easier place for gamers to start.

A wonderful example of relationship building through MMORPGs is the countless stories you often hear of players meeting each other through the game and eventually getting married in real life. This phenomenon has been around long enough that we are now seeing the kids of these couples playing in the same game as their parents. These are digital worlds, yet they still provide a very valid place to experience and practice real relationships.

Where there are deeper commitments to games, there can be deeper relationships formed. Experiencing friction and overcoming hurdles together can sometimes make the best bonds. Given the barriers and constraints MMORPGs face, the entry level to a social guild or community-focused one, rather than a raid group, is more accessible for these types of games. Though when considering raid groups, it is also a very quick way to form bonds and relationships with others.

Raid groups, however, are probably more common, and to join one, I would recommend understanding the gameplay meta in order to easily synchronize with the groups you find to play with. If you have challenging quests you need to conquer within a team environment, you will find plenty of opportunities to resolve conflicts through *nemawashi* or build stronger bonds through *guanxi*.

2. Understanding what Bad Looks Like

Military Simulation games, like *Hell Let Loose* or *Squad,* have community-based servers that make it a little easier to build relationships with other players. It's more persistent and steady, where you can keep coming back to their server, and once you see the same players over and over again, bonds can be formed. Some community-hosted servers post their websites or Discord channels as soon as players join, giving players another place to meet and interact.

Even with that community support, the nature of public servers also results in an inconsistent player base, making practicing conflict resolution a little harder than in MMORPGs. Instead of giant servers, these games usually have servers that can support 100 people at a time. So there might be a queue system before more players can join, and it can't always be the same 100 people each time. This can make it more difficult to form bonds with other gamers versus being in a guild-type community.

What I really enjoy about these game types, though, is how

often I see how poor relationship building occurs through wrong leadership styles. These types of games ask players to step up and lead, and unfortunately, some gamers have never experienced leadership. Some gamers think leadership is what you see in Hollywood movies, with someone who can fire off quick orders and get everyone listening and organized.

I have seen in-game leaders just join teams and start barking orders like Captain America, and they expect everyone to fall in line. 80% of the time, I would say the lobby or gamers revolt and start yelling at them to shut up. There is no way you are going to be able to build relationships with other gamers if you can't read the room. You need to be able to tell what team you are working with and who those people are as individuals. Maybe they were perfectly okay with the commands and instructions, but it was just the tone of voice that made it unacceptable.

In some of my prior examples, I have shown how coercive leadership from guild leaders in *Guild Wars 2* was a lesson in how not to lead, because their leadership style directly impacted their relationships with the team. You can't lead without followers, and if there are followers and leaders, there is a relationship between them that needs to be managed.

The more you can witness good and poor examples of leadership, the more data you can build in your mind to understand how relationships play out. If you just want to learn about the game itself, pay attention to the people who do well and note what they did. Did they build relationships with other people in the game, and did the other gamers resonate with them?. Make note of when the other gamers revolt and hate when someone else is giving instructions. Try to diagnose why it failed and what you would have done differently to handle the situation.

Find some community servers with good ping or latency, and make sure you continue to just keep going back to the same one. What other teams, communities, or clans play in those servers? Do you notice the same people chatting and discussing gameplay in the chat? Those are easy ways to find the consistent playerbase associated with those games.

It's no different than finding a community softball league or any other type of team in the physical world. Repetition and consistency are the keys to those relationships and build a base upon which bonds can form easily. The games with these types of servers should be a key indicator that these skills can be practiced.

3. Simulating relationships

The Sims Series is such a wonderful example when talking about the simulation genre. It's the human experience mirrored to its best effort in the digital world. There are even more defined experiences with different levels of complexity. Growing up, there were the *Tamagotchi pets,* where you had to feed this digital pet that you carried around on a keychain. Today, there are single-player games that are extremely story-driven, so much so that you are bought into the fictional relationship between characters, just like you would be in a movie or TV show. Even on Steam, there are many dating sims where players engage in conversational games with digital avatars.

While I would recommend practicing relationship-building skills with other physical gamers, it still feels important to note that if you don't want to play online games, there are still other options to pull from. I think that if you can take the moral high ground in your decisions with NPCs, and go the extra mile to be a servant leader for them, that's how you become a Maslow's Producer.

If you want to take the opposite approach and see what poor decisions look like, that is also more forgiving in these playstyles.

Let's try not feeding your digital pets and see how that turns out. In any conversation with an NPC, say the most insulting option available. If you are in front of an NPC, can you attack them in-game? If it is possible, what usually happens after you attack them? You can still practice and analyze relationship skills in this context.

Most games are based on the real world, so why would the computers in these games be any different? We know the right and wrong choices and how they might impact relationships, and with those computers or NPCs, we shouldn't be that surprised with our results. When you play these games, you need to pause to consider what might happen before you choose your next action. Then see if you were right or wrong based on the results, and ask yourself why.

However, the last struggle with a simulation genre game is that practicing *nemawashi* and *guanxi* are just not really possible with computers or NPCs. These skills require negotiating and aligning with unique perspectives to reach decisions, or building deep relationship bonds that mature over time and commitment. I'm not saying this possibility doesn't exist in a simulation game, or won't in the future, but I am unaware of any currently. If you have a good simulation game where those two skills can be practiced, then do it.

For minor examples, you can see *guanxi* in action in RPG games, like in the NPC village story discussed earlier, where everyone in town was in love with my friend's warrior. These relationships are often too one-sided to fully practice the art of guanxi, as the game design around these encounters is very straightforward. It's usually a literal quest system where "Player does function A," and the game world "Will give player new special treatment X." This is worth noting, but will be a less nuanced scenario in which to practice relationship building for yourself with real people.

Games are consistently evolving, and who knows where the era of A.I. will take us. Even now, we see ChatGPT, Grok, and Gemini as the main A.I. brands and tools people use around the world. The language model and ability for NPCs and computers to have greater conversations with you is only around the corner, and is already being tested in games like *Fortnite*. Now, when we want special treatment of persistent relationships with our NPC counterparts, maybe A.I. will solve that.

Any game that gives players more tools and in-depth knowledge of the world is a big win in my opinion. I look forward to seeing how computer and NPC advancements bring a new wave of features for all players to enjoy and practice from.

Key Lessons:

Lesson to be learned	Objective while playing in a game
Joining a team.	Work with strangers in competitive and cooperative games. Adjust your communication approach based on different team members' needs and personalities.
Building a positive reputation.	Engage with player communities and observe how reputation influences group dynamics. Use servant leadership, accountability, and compassion to earn a good reputation.
Earning *guanxi* with others, the power of relationships.	Build consistent behaviors with others that turn into relationships. Identify what types of values you can earn from others by being a kind person to them, looking for nothing in return.
Practicing harmonious decision-making with *Nemawashi*.	When there is conflict in a game you are playing, or a resolution needs to be identified, see if *Nemawashi* can be used to make decision-making smoother.

Bonus tips for a positive reputation with respect to accountability and compassion:

1. Set clear expectations.

2. Follow up and follow through.

3. Provide encouragement and feedback by celebrating victories.

4. Facilitate open communication.

5. Respect boundaries.

6. Lead by example.

7. Adjust strategies as needed.

Mission Briefing

Find a game with a team, guild, or squad structure. Create your own team and invite others to join it.

1. You will need to establish:

2. What is your name and identity?

3. What are your goals and objectives?

4. What is your structure?

5. What are your culture and policies?

6. What types of members and roles do you want to join?

7. Recruit like-minded individuals.

Once you have established these things, how can you solidify them and lead by example so that others will follow?

To be successful, you must be able to complete the goals and objectives.

WHAT'S NEXT?

If you were looking for more information on how to be a video game producer, I hope this can be your first step in recognizing that you are already on your way there through the games you play. If you are already a video game producer, I hope these lessons shed some light on how another fellow producer thinks about their craft. And, if you just wanted to see how video games could be applied to your personal life, school, or career, I hope these stories were understandable and relatable.

It's important to discuss what this book lacked and did not set you up for success in. It did not deep dive into specific game development processes or terminology on purpose. Different types of game studios and producers use different terminology and definitions for certain things. We did not discuss game development roadmap terminology like "Development Complete," "Polish Complete," or "Code Lock." We did not discuss the importance of playtesting and feedback loops. I wanted to avoid defining what it meant to hit an Alpha versus a Beta milestone. I wanted the skills discussed and the idea of the Game Intuitive Mindset to enable producers to take on any type of team and challenge, as this is going to consistently evolve.

We also did not look at the incredible wealth of knowledge in project task structure and task management tools like *Jira*, *Asana*, and *Monday*. As you will learn, some producers have different ways they want to structure tasks in parent and child structures. This is a hierarchical way to break tasks down, with child tasks grouped under a single parent task. With different tools having different systems for users to organize and label them, there was no point in going through the different options. We did address this in a subtle way during the discussion on being a production taskmaster. If you can read an advanced-level guide and be able to mimic its structure, you can create a project plan in any type of software.

As video games become more advanced, the specialization of the producer will likely continue to advance with it. There will be new tools, techniques, and terms that will also continue to advance. Fundamentals are far more important than discussing concepts that will likely age out of date.

If you would like to increase your knowledge in certain areas, there are several places to get further education. The *Project Management Institute (PMI)* is an organization that I have a ton of respect for. I even have one of their certifications, the *Project Management Professional (PMP)*. They have the best terminology for processes that is more universal for Project Management across multiple industries like health, government, industrial, and military. I think if you are absolutely interested in at least the field of project management or production, you should consider looking into it.

Additionally, there are several Scrum certification organizations that might come and go, but the *Certified Scrum Master (CSM)* is valuable and attractive to most teams. There are many free and low effort costs to investigate these certifications, like watching YouTube videos and following influencers on social media who talk about the lessons and principles. The goal is not just to fully follow their processes, but to become more well-rounded and a true servant leader to the team. You want to grow stronger outside of video games, and additional learning is the best way to gain an understanding of other types of teams. I would encourage you to continue your video game producer education in any way that interests you.

My goal was to try to teach these concepts in a different way, in a way that worked for me, and maybe a way that might work for you. I've always been a visual learner and wished there was more content for learning skills and abilities in project management. Video game experiences were always the analogies I liked to share, and I saw that my fellow gamers often understood exactly what I meant.

When I first started learning project management principles and applying them to the digital teams I played with, it opened up Pandora's box. I started to get a glimpse into how systems and mechanics work together, in a way that no one seemed to be talking about. There was an entire profession and career path focused on this, yet I couldn't find anyone making the connections I wanted to see.

There have been many books on "gamification" and how to build job systems with a game design mindset. There are books on how to make games and ones focused on game development. But there haven't been any books about how to be a video game producer on a game development team. Now there is one.

I was determined that if I was going to write a book about video game production and what it means to be a video game producer, it had to be done through the lens of video games. It's extremely rare to come across someone in the game industry who is a producer and has never played a video game. These stories may come from a different time period for some, but the moral of the stories should still apply.

The wisdom I tried to share comes from the many friends and

gamers I've played with who share this love of video games. I've tried to take those experiences and shape them into something more relatable. Hopefully, I've shown that you can connect the video game industry with your favorite pastime. Hopefully, you've noticed that being a gamer has taught you valuable skills that translate to the real world. That was truly my intention.

Take the lessons I have provided and apply them to be a good producer in this industry. I hope you understand what I mean by leadership and managing now, instead of just using soft or hard skills. Servant leadership is the key to everything that we do. You have been practicing these skills this entire time.

If you, as a gamer, feel even slightly more confident, or if this inspired you to lead in games, then I'll feel like I did my job. Life should be fun. Games should be fun. And the way we learn and think should be fun. Enjoy, and play more games.

Speaking of playing more games. Have you ever wondered what it would be like to be a Video Game Designer? Have you ever wondered how some of the best games in the world have a design that keeps you engaged and having fun? How can you apply those video game designs and mechanics to your real life? If you have wondered about that, like I have, maybe check out TheVideoGameDesigner.com. Signup on the email list and be prepared for the next lesson in your training.

Bash 'em

Fin

ACKNOWLEDGEMENTS

There are hundreds of people who have influenced my work and opinions on these topics, and that is far too many to thank and shout out. First and foremost, thank you to my wife, Danielle, who has always supported my efforts to write a book when I never thought I could. Thank you, Evan and Jason, to whom this book is dedicated, for being the perfect people to write for. Every story and lesson I hope will bring a smile to your face and show how my Caseyisms are coming through the pages. I wrote every story for you two, and it's okay that you will never read them, because you lived them.

My mother-in-law, Sharon, was one of the first people to ever read the book, and she gave me the confidence that it made sense and that I am actually able to write. My friends Melanie and Lindsey pushed me to be more inclusive to other types of readers and to make sure my voice comes through stronger. Thank you.

My closest friends helped read the book and gave me early feedback on what was wrong. Aaron, thank you for all your insight and feedback, and for listening to me work through my ideas while we are out surfing. Devin, Jonas, Josh, and Mike, I am very grateful that every time we hung out, you never shut me down when I tried to talk about the book and always helped where needed. Nick and Kelly, a special thanks for helping me work through the creative efforts of the book's design. Brad, your kind words and excitement were very helpful in telling me how much you could relate to my stories.

To all my friends not listed who had an early copy of the book, thank you for putting up with me and listening to me rant, and trying to get folks to read it. The fact that you all showed interest and support is all I could ever ask for. Thank you.

To my many other team members from all the various game studios I have worked for who shared some of these stories with me, thank you. To the people who helped me grow after tense or tight development deadlines and overtime, thank you. To all the other mentors, thought leaders, and professors who wrote materials around team management and leadership, thank you.

Most importantly, I honestly believe this book wouldn't even be half as good without the support of my editor, Emily. I needed a friend who could help me polish this book up, someone who knew how to talk about games in a fun and light way that could match my style, and she knocked it out of the park. Emily, thank you from the bottom of my heart for how well you made my book better by helping me add more personal stories and connect my thoughts together in a nice flow.

I couldn't have done this by myself and am grateful that I have so many supportive friends. Thank you.

REFERENCES

- Beck, K., Beedle, M. A., van Bennekum, A., Cockburn, A., Cunningham, W., Fowler, M., Grenning, J., & Highsmith, J. (2001). *Manifesto for agile software development.* Retrieved January 30, 2025, from https://agilemanifesto.org

- Bennis, Warren G. (2009). *On Becoming a Leader.* Basic Books.

- Cialdini, R. B. (2007). *Influence: The Psychology of Persuasion.* HarperCollins.

- George, M. (2003). *Lean Six Sigma for service: How to use lean speed and Six Sigma quality to improve services and transactions.* McGraw-Hill.

- Greenleaf, R. (n.d.). *What is Servant Leadership. Greenleaf Center for Servant Leadership.* Retrieved January 30, 2025, from https://www.greenleaf.org/what-is-servant-leadership/

- Greenleaf, R. K. (2016). *The Power of Servant Leadership.* Brilliance Publishing.

- Herzberg, F., Mausner, B., & Snyderman, B. B. (1959). *The motivation to work* (2nd ed.). New York, NY: John Wiley & Sons.

- Maslow, A. H. (1943). A theory of human motivation. *Psychological Review, 50*(4), 370–396. https://doi.org/10.1037/h0054346

- McChrystal, S. A., Collins, T., Silverman, D., & Fussell, C. (2015). *Team of teams: New rules of engagement for a complex world.*

Portfolio/Penguin.

- Meier, S. (2021). *Sid Meier's memoir! A life in computer games.* W. W. Norton & Company.

- Ouchi, W. G. (1981). *Theory Z: How American business can meet the Japanese challenge.* Reading, MA: Addison-Wesley.

- Royce, W. (1970, August). *Managing the Development of large software systems.* In *Proceedings of IEEE WESCON.* Retrieved from https://www.semanticscholar.org/paper/Managing-the-development-of-large-software-systems%3A-Royce/e0983a9d-430ba4775ec1b9ee8c460a5a5994f9b8

- Schwaber, K. (1997). *Scrum Development Process.* In J. Sutherland, C. Casanave, J. Miller, J. Patel, & G. Hollowell (Eds.), *Business object design and implementation* (pp. 117–134).

- Spears, L. C. (1995). *Reflections on Leadership: How Robert K. Greenleaf's theory of servant-leadership influenced today's top management thinkers.* New York: John Wiley & Sons.

- Takeuchi, H., & Nonaka, I. (1986, January). *The New Product Development Game. Harvard Business Review.* Retrieved from https://hbr.org/1986/01/the-new-new-product-development-game

- International Game Developers Association. (2023). *Developer satisfaction survey.* Retrieved January 30, 2025, from https://igda.org/news-archive/press-release-the-igda-and-western-university-release-2023-developer-satisfaction-survey/

- Carcich, B. (Host). (n.d.). *Building Better Games* Podcast. Retrieved January 30, 2025.

www.ingramcontent.com/pod-product-compliance
Lightning Source LLC
Chambersburg PA
CBHW051305130726
47987CB00004B/1669